JUDAISM SPEAKS
TO THE MODERN WORLD

BY THE SAME AUTHOR:

The Jewish Law of Agency: With Special Reference to the Roman and the Common Law

Steering or Drifting — Which?

Judaism — An Analysis and an Interpretation

A New World Is Born

Point of View — An Analysis of American Judaism

ISRAEL H. LEVINTHAL

JUDAISM SPEAKS TO THE MODERN WORLD

RAM'S
HORN
BOOKS

ABELARD-SCHUMAN
London New York Toronto

Library of Congress Catalogue
Card Number: 63-18670

LONDON	NEW YORK	TORONTO
Abelard-Schuman	Abelard-Schuman	Abelard-Schuman
Limited	Limited	Canada Limited
8 King St. WC 2	6 West 57th St.	896 Queen St. W.

Printed in the United States of America

To the memory of
my revered and beloved father
RABBI DOV ARYEH LEVINTHAL
Baal halakah uvaal haggadah
Master of Jewish Law and Jewish Lore

CONTENTS

JUDAISM SPEAKS
TO THE MODERN WORLD

Introduction

In the Boston Public Library, as part of the mural decorations depicting the history of religion, by the American artist John S. Sargent, there are two paintings; one entitled *The Church*, the other *The Synagogue*. The former is portrayed as a young, blooming woman, vibrant with beauty and vigor; the latter as an old, blind, decrepit woman, with disheveled hair and no trace of pristine comeliness.

These paintings, when originally placed in the Library Gallery in 1919, aroused considerable controversy and a wave of protest among the leaders of American Jewry as well as among liberal Christians. Sargent, however, was merely representing a view held by most Christians in the medieval ages and by many Christians even now. A modern historian, Arnold J. Toynbee, describes Judaism as an outworn civilization which, though it may have had a message for the world in the days of its youth, has, since the advent of Christianity, become a fossil, bereft of significance or value for mankind today.

This concept, of course, is a gross libel against Judaism. The evidence is comprehensive and clear that Judaism has never lost its vitality and that it is still a potent and influential force for good in the world. The great and extensive Rabbinic literature, which continues the tradition of the Bible and has flourished continuously from Biblical times to this very day — a literature familiar to many Christian scholars — furnishes elo-

11

quent testimony that Judaism has ever spoken meaningfully
to mankind and that it has a much-needed and precious message for modern man.

Life today, to be sure, is much different from and more
complex than in the days of the ancient Rabbis; and, naturally, we cannot expect to find in their teachings specific answers
addressed precisely to the many novel or peculiar problems
which face men and nations today. But these sages in Jewish
history, with their keen and fertile minds, with their profound
understanding of human nature and experience, possessed an
inexhaustible reservoir of rich spiritual insights not restricted
to time or place. Theirs was a deep and broad wisdom which is
applicable in all generations and which can immeasurably
benefit mankind. This is the glory of Judaism — that its teachings are eternally valid, and that its message, though most ancient, is also most modern.

To the Rabbis, the Torah was ever-living and always unfold-
ing new truths. These men had the remarkable faculty of being able to discover the deeper meaning of the words of the
Bible. As the classic work of Jewish mysticism, the *Zohar*, ex-
presses it: "Woe to the one who thinks that the Bible's purpose is just to relate stories or tales about men or events;
these tales are but the garb with which the Torah clothes lofty
thoughts and ideas. Just as the garment which one wears is not
to be mistaken for the real person, which is his living soul, so,
too, must these tales not be regarded as the real essence or soul
of the Torah — that essence or soul is the Divine truth imbed-
ded within these words. This is what the Psalmist meant, when
he prayed: 'Open Thou mine eyes that I may behold wondrous
things out of Thy Torah.' "[1]

It was the unique greatness of the Rabbis that they could
see and reveal the "wondrous things" which the Torah offered
as a guide for all men in all ages. They express these deeper in-

1) Zohar, *Behaalotka*; Psalms, 119:18.

sights through their own *agadot*, tales and legends, maxims and aphorisms, scattered in the classic works of the Talmud and Midrash. These *agadot* are beacons of light illuminating the paths of life for mankind and enabling men and women, if their eyes are open and their hearts receptive, to discover abundant spiritual treasure.

It was the purpose and the task of the Jewish preacher in past centuries to utilize these beacons for the benefit of his brethren. He discussed every problem facing the Jew and mankind, and found not only inspiration but also interpretation and solution for the problem in the brilliant teachings of the Rabbis. The preacher thus kept alive the spirit and message of Judaism, applying the Biblical and Rabbinic insights to the needs and interests of his generation.

It is often said that sermons are to be spoken or heard, not published or read. This view may be true regarding sermons which, in reality, are merely oral editorials, expressing opinions as a newspaper would on current events or problems. It was not true, however, regarding the *Jewish* sermon — the *d'rush* — as customarily delivered in the past. That type of sermon was *Torah*, part of the tradition which furnished a new and fresh container for the old wine of Jewish wisdom. *Sifre d'rush* — volumes of Jewish sermons — were published and they formed a respected portion of the books in the home of the intelligent Jewish layman as well as in the library of the Rabbi. Even in recent times such publications have been popular, works by such preachers as Adolf Jellinek and N.P. Chajes, of Vienna, Ezekiel Libshitz, the head of the Polish Rabbinate, Isaac Nissenbaum, of Poland, and Mosheh A. Amiel, of Tel Aviv. The public has found in their many editions new revelations of the Torah, fresh interpretations of Judaism offering guidance as well as novel insights into life.

These expositions of our Torah have not been addressed to the Jew alone. They have been an enlightenment to all peoples. Rabbi Jeremiah, a sage who lived at the beginning of the fourth century of our common era, interpreting the words: *Zot Torat haadam,* "This is the Torah of man,"[2] tells us: "The Torah is not the Torah of the priests, nor the Torah of the Levites, nor the Torah of the Israelites, but the Torah of Man!"[3] This is still our conviction, that Judaism speaks to all men and has a universal message for all time.

It is in the spirit of these views that I offer in this volume a number of my sermons and addresses. In a most modest way, I have ventured to follow the tradition of the classic Jewish preachers of the past and hope that I have fulfilled, in some measure, their ideals of the Jewish sermon.

*   *   *   *

I acknowledge my gratitude to my son-in-law, Mr. Lester Lyons, of the New York Bar, and to my son, Mr. Lazar E. Levinthal, for their kindness in reading the manuscript and for their many valuable suggestions and helpful criticisms in the preparation of this volume. I thank Mrs. Elias N. Rabinowitz for her labors in typing the entire manuscript. To the men and women of the Brooklyn Jewish Center I express a special debt for the stimulation I have received from the keen interest ever displayed by them in my humble efforts to transmit the teachings of Judaism. It was Walt Whitman who said: "To have great poets there must be great audiences too."[4] That observation is similarly applicable to preaching. I have been blessed with a congregation whose love and appreciation of the traditional Jewish sermon has brought out the best within me. To my beloved wife, I acknowledge my greatest obligation, for it is to her congenial exhortations and constant inspiration that the publication of this volume is largely due.

I conclude with a devout prayer of thankfulness to our Heav-

2) II Samuel, 7:19.
3) Sifra, (ed. I. H. Weiss, Vienna, 1862), p. 86b.
4) Quoted by Alfred A. Knopf, *Atlantic Monthly,* (December, 1957).

enly Father that I was able to complete this work and to present it for publication on the eve of my seventy-fifth birthday. I pray that I may be granted health and strength to continue to delve into the "wondrous things" of our Torah and to impart them to my people and to others for years to come.
Shevat 12, 5723.
February 6, 1963.

I. H. L

Prefatory Note

In quoting Hebrew words or phrases, I have used as simple a transliteration in English as possible. The following letters have been used in this connection: *ch*, for the *chet*; *k*, for the *chaf*; *t* for the *sav* and the *tav*.

All the sermons and addresses, unless otherwise specified, were delivered from the pulpit of the Brooklyn Jewish Center.

Most of the sermons are printed in the length delivered. Some appear in shortened form, because of the omission of illustrations or ideas that were merely of transient value, or of thoughts already expressed in other sermons. In all cases I have tried to retain the style of the spoken word, and have foregone attempts at literary embellishment.

A few sermons, namely, "Amalek and Haman — A Study in Contrast," "The Ten Plagues and Their Modern Significance," and "The Prophet Ezekiel's Message to a Modern World Struggling for Freedom," refer to disturbing events now happily passed. They are included, however, for their historical importance and as an admonition against the possible repetition of such events.

I realize that it is not always wise to record in a volume such as this an appraisal of a living person in high elective office. Nevertheless, I have included a sermon dealing with President Kennedy because I believe both the subject and the applicable Jewish interpretation are important enough to warrant it.

I. H. L

The Upsurge of Religion
and the Ethical Climate in America

Preached on Yom Kippur,
September 21, 1961

A very interesting observation was recently made by a distinguished Christian theologian, the president of the Union Theological Seminary in New York, Dr. Henry Van Dusen. Addressing the General Assembly of the United Presbyterian Church on the subject of the present revived interest in religion which seems manifest in all America, he called attention to a strange paradox. "The return to religion in our day," he said, "has produced no corresponding moral fruitage. On the contrary, while the curve of religious interest has been rising, that of moral health has been falling. Here is the most profound contradiction in our national existence — steadily rising attention to religion, steadily declining ethical practice. ... It is precisely at the moment of largest adherence to religious loyalties and religious institutions in its history that the nation's life is marked by a disintegration in moral and ethical behavior."

I feel certain that this is an observation which many of us have made. Religious institutions boast today of the largest memberships they have ever had. This is true of the Synagogue as well as the Church, especially in the suburban communities. Multimillion dollar Houses of Worship are being erected throughout the land. There seems to be an upsurge in our religious life. As Dr. Van Dusen put it, "the curve of religious interest has been rising," leading many people to

19

think that America is now experiencing a religious revival. And yet, this return "has produced no corresponding moral fruitage." On the contrary, the curve of our ethical conduct has fallen to a low degree. Wherever we turn we see evidences of ethical and even moral disintegration.

I am not speaking now of the ordinary criminal, the product of slum, broken home, lack of education or derangement of mind. This is a problem in itself, worthy of the serious attention of the criminologist and the sociologist. I am instead referring to men who occupy responsible positions in our social, political, and economic life, men who are looked up to as leaders in their communities, who are church-going and active in their religious affiliations. Hardly a day passes that our newspapers do not disclose corrupt practices and violations of moral standards by men occupying positions of trust in every sector of the community. And these are men who not only lay claim to religious affiliation but also profess to take their religion seriously.

At the recent trials of the high officials of several of our country's largest corporations, at which they were being charged with violations of statutes regulating business conduct, nearly all of the defendants brought character witnesses who testified that the defendants were members of religious denominations and even occupied high positions in their respective churches.

A few months ago, *Time* magazine published an extract of an interesting article which had appeared in the *Harvard Business Review*, written by Rev. Raymond C. Baumhart, S. J., a doctoral student at the Harvard Business School, who was making a study of the ethical climate of American business today. He had circularized 1700 business executives throughout the land, asking for their frank evaluation of the ethical standards they had found to be in vogue among the people of their trade. The answers he received are revealing and distressing. Four out of five in the survey said that one or more unethical practices are "common" in their fields. Among the practices cited were price-fixing and bribery. "The average business man would countenance padding of expense accounts, raiding other companies' employees to learn top secrets." Asked who in their opinion was to blame, most executives pointed to top management. And here again it must be emphasized that these violators of moral principles are closely identified with their denominational organizations and would profess to be religious.

How, then, can we explain this paradox, this contrast between religious protestation and actual disregard for religious and ethical practice? The answer is simple. These people misconceive the real meaning and purpose of religion. They do not associate religion with ethics. They do not understand that religion demands a transformation of our whole life, that it seeks to influence every aspect of our daily activities and that its principal function is to mold us into moral beings.

Religion has become a matter of formality and conformity; church-going is the proper thing for one to do. It becomes a matter of social practice and usage. Or, at best, people look upon religion as the performance of certain rites that we owe to God, to pay Him a weekly call at His House, to recite a few prayers and to listen politely to a sermon. It is something necessary for Saturday or Sunday, but not for the rest of the week; something that applies to the church, not to the market place, factory, or conference room.

This view is not new in the history of religion. The prophets in ancient Israel railed against this misconception of religion. Jeremiah decried the attitude of many in his day who violated every ethical and moral precept and who thought that their perfunctory attendance to the ritual of the Temple was all that religion required of them, people who cried, "The Temple of the Lord, the Temple of the Lord, the Temple of the Lord,"[1]

1) Jeremiah, 7:4-5.

as if no more were essential. (Parenthetically, Jews of today should take note of the meaningful interpretation given by the great commentator, Rashi, to this triple cry, "Temple of the Lord." He explained, "The people referred to their visit at the Temple on three occasions in the year," the implication being that that alone was enough.) Jeremiah's thunderous reply is as valid today as it was in his day: "Nay, but if ye thoroughly amend your ways and your doings; if ye thoroughly execute justice between man and man!"

This is the real tragedy of our so-called religious revival, a tragedy that affects the well-being of our national life. We have lost the sense of moral values, and, what is worse, we have divorced religion from its very essence, the ethical life. Everything is permitted as long as one is not found out. There is no shame in wrongdoing. The only shame experienced today is, again to quote the prophet Jeremiah, "the shame of the thief *ki yimatze*, when he is caught."[2]

It is this misconception and misrepresentation of religion that has alienated many fine and sensitive souls, turning them away from religion altogether. A brilliant professor of philosophy at Princeton University, Dr. Walter A. Kaufmann, in his recently published book, *The Faith of a Heretic*, gives as one of the reasons for his loss of interest in organized religion the failure of religion to produce morality. With all due respect to the learned professor, I must say that this failure is not inherent in religion, but is the fault of many of its co-called adherents, who, alas, by their actions, falsify the true meaning of religion.

Certainly, for Jews, it is impossible to think of religion without its ethical imperatives. It is interesting to note on the Day of Atonement — when we come before the Lord to plead for forgiveness — that we are told by the Rabbis in the Talmud, "the Day of Atonement atones only for our failures in our duties to God, but does not atone for our transgressions to-

2) *Ibid.* 2:26.

wards our fellow man, until we have first made good the wrong done to him."[3]

Again, take note, that on this very day when we refrain from all food and drink, the prophetic lesson assigned for the Scriptural reading at the Synagogue service is the message of Isaiah: "Is this the fast that I have chosen? Is it to spread ashes and sackcloth under you? Wilt thou call this a fast, and an acceptable day to the Lord?"[4] The prophet certainly did not oppose the Torah injunction to fast and to afflict one's soul on this solemn day. But he understood its true meaning, that it was not an end in itself, but only a means of reaching the highest demands of the moral life. Alas, he saw how many had misconceived the function of the fast: "Behold, in the day of your fast ye pursue your business, and harshly compel full payment. Behold, ye fast in strife and contention, and smite with the fist of wickedness. . . . Is not this the fast that I have chosen? To loose the fetters of wickedness!" In these ringing words of the prophet we find expressed the true meaning and function of religion, to "break every yoke" which keeps us from living according to the highest ideals of the ethical and moral life.

The Rabbis, too, continue this emphasis on the moral implications of religion. "Why did God engrave the Ten Commandments on two tablets of stone and not on one?" asks a Rabbi. And he answers, "To teach us that the five commands on the first tablet are *k'neged shamayim*, duties to God in heaven, whereas the five on the second tablet speak of earthly duties, *k'neged eretz*, those that we owe to our fellow man."[5] Both are of equally Divine sanction.

One of the finest statements in all religious literature is the one made by a Rabbi in the Talmud who tells us that "the first question man is asked when he appears before the Throne of God's Judgment is: *Nasata v'natatah b'emunah*, Have you

3) Mishnah Yoma, 8:9.
4) Isaiah, ch. 58.
5) Exodus Rabbah, 41:7.

dealt honorably and faithfully, in all your dealings with your fellow man?"[6] What a revealing insight into the Hebraic concept of true religion!

Commenting on the Psalmist's words: "I shall walk before the Lord in the lands of the living,"[7] the Rabbis tell us that "lands of the living — *zeh makom shevakim* — refer to the market places,"[8] this is where man must walk before the Lord!

Perhaps the most telling illustration of the role religion should play in guiding our ethical thoughts and actions is the story that the Talmud tells of the sage, Simeon ben Shetach. He had purchased an ass from an Ishmaelite, and on the following day had discovered a precious jewel entwined around the animal's neck. When his friends heard of the good fortune that had befallen the Rabbi, they rushed to him and said: "This is God's blessing to you; you will now be rich!" But the Rabbi was quick to respond: "I purchased an ass, I did not purchase the jewel. I must return the jewel to its owner!" His friends protested that the Ishmaelite evidently meant the jewel to go with the purchase, and that the Rabbi therefore had the right to keep it. "What think ye of me; am I a barbarian?" was his retort, and hurriedly he returned the jewel to the Ishmaelite. At this, the Ishmaelite cried out: "Blessed be the God of Simeon; blessed be the God of the Jews!"[9]

These were not simply abstract teachings of particular idealists; they reflect the norms of Jewish religious life, the standards of ethical conduct which the average Jew knew were the demands of his religion. As Dr. Emil G. Hirsch, a noted Reform Jewish preacher of a generation ago, put it: "The Jew never tolerated the assumption that one may be *frum* and still morally *crum*," that one may be pious and still morally corrupt! On the contrary, Judaism teaches that a man who exhib-

6) Shabbat, 31a.
7) Psalms, 116:9.
8) Yoma, 71a.
9) Tal. Jer. Baba Metzia, II:5; Deuteronomy Rabbah, 3:5.

its allegiance to religious affiliation and observance of religious rites is deemed to warrant his scrupulous adherence to ethical principles in his conduct. The Talmud tells of a man who entrusted a sum of money to a person who was wearing the *tefillin*, the phylactories which an observant Jew wears for his morning prayers. Later, when the man asked for the return of the money, the wearer of the *tefillin* refused to return it, even denying that he had ever received it. The man, pleading for his money, said: "I had confidence in the *tefillin* which you wore."[10] The man was correct. The *tefillin* worn by the observant Jew should have been sufficient guarantee of his honesty in his dealings with his fellow men.

And because Judaism exemplifies this concept of religion, it behooves American Jews to be in the forefront of those who strive to translate religious teachings to the ethical conduct of daily life. We owe this to ourselves as Jews, in order to glorify the name of God. And we owe this to America, the land we cherish. Historians have shown us that many great and powerful empires have disintegrated through moral decay. If America is to thrive and to blossom, and if religion is to serve America's national life, then religion must be true to its noblest purpose and, like the sap which penetrates every part of the tree, religion must penetrate every phase of our daily lives.

Only thus will this present so-called religious upsurge have genuine significance and prove to be a vivifying force in our individual and national life.

10) Jerusalem Talmud, Berakot, 2:3.

Judaism
and Human Brotherhood

Preached Saturday, February 18, 1961,
during Brotherhood Week.

The Torah reading prescribed for this Sabbath is particularly appropriate today when the people of the United States are observing Brotherhood Week. It is a good idea to stress the theme of human brotherhood in the period between the celebrations of the birthdays of Washington and Lincoln; for it was the dream and hope of both the founder and the preserver of our Republic that in this land all men should enjoy the blessings of freedom and liberty and should regard each other as brothers.

Alas, the ideal of human brotherhood has not yet taken hold in the spirits of all men. Evidently something more is required than merely assigning one week in the year for its observance. What is needed is a transformation of our understanding of religion and of what religion demands of us.

I would like to review with you the Jewish attitude to see what message Judaism has to offer to a world struggling to attain this ideal. Our Bible emphasizes again and again the great truth of the brotherhood of man. Vividly summarizing the theme uppermost in the minds of the ancient prophets is the verse, "Have we not all one Father, hath not one God created us all? Why do we deal treacherously every man against his brother?"[1] And even earlier, Abraham, the father of our people and our faith, had pleaded with Lot for the

1) Malaki, 2:10.

avoidance of quarrel and disunity: "Let there be no strife between me and thee . . . for we are brothers!"[2]

The Torah lesson of this Sabbath, however, goes into more detail on this subject, and graphically describes the important steps that man must take in order eventually to achieve the goal of the fellowship of man. It is a message that the world may gravely consider today.

Our Torah reading tells the story of God's command to Moses, which he was to convey to the Israelites, to build a *mishkan*, a sanctuary, and gives the details of its construction and its furnishings. This sanctuary was to bring home to the people the message of their Torah and thus to bring God closer to them. "And let them make me a sanctuary that I may dwell *in the midst of them*,"[3] God said to Moses. This, then, is the function of religion, which the House of God was to symbolize, to make God dwell in man's heart and mind.

The most important item of that sacred building was to be the Ark, which was to contain the tablets of God's Law. Its construction is described in great detail. Above the Ark was to be the *kaporet*, the ark-cover, the design of which is explicitly described: "And thou shalt make two cherubim of gold . . . at the two ends of the ark-cover. And thou shalt make one cherub at the one end, and one cherub at the other end, and at the two ends thereof. . . . And the wings of the cherubim shall be spread upwards, with their faces *ish el achiv*, one toward the other,"[4] literally, each toward his brother!

Here, in just three sentences, we have, in essence, the true function of religion which the House of God was to convey to the entering worshiper.

Like the wings of the cherubim, which were to be spread *l'maalah* — upward — so, too, when we enter the sanctuary, our thoughts, our minds, our hearts, should turn upward, to seek

2) Genesis, 13:8.
3) Exodus, 25:8.
4) *Ibid.*, 25:18-20.

closer contact with our Divine Father, and to commune with
Him in what Martin Buber has so beautifully described as
the "I and Thou dialogue."

But religion, and the sanctuary which symbolizes it, must
not stop there. The text continues: "And their faces shall be
turned *ish el achiv,* each to his brother." Here is the vital
element of religion, without which religion can have neither
meaning nor relevance in our lives. It is not enough for man
— even at frequent intervals — to attune his mind upward,
Heavenward; but, like the faces of the cherubim which were
turned each to its brother, so, too, our heavenly thoughts
must inspire us and direct us to turn our faces to our brothers.

Tragedy lies in mankind's failure to grasp this basic concept of religion. Men go to church and to synagogue, and
momentarily turn their thoughts upward; but they stop there
and suppose nothing more is required of them. They miss the
all-important truth which the cherubim should convey to us,
that we must look to our fellow man and regard him as our
brother. Unless we do this, even if our eyes are turned to the
House of God, we fail to follow the Will of God.[5]

Our text pursues the theme further. The Rabbis noticed
something strange in the use of one word in the Hebrew text
of the Biblical passage: "And thou shalt make *sh'neiyim keru-
vim,* two cherubim." The use of the word *sh'neiyim* is very
odd. True, this word does mean the numeral "two," but only if
used by itself, without a noun following. In Hebrew grammar,
the rule is that the word *shnay* is to be used when the numeral
two is connected with a noun in a descriptive manner. Many
instances in the Bible will illustrate this rule.[6] Here, however,
we are struck by what seems to be an exception to the general
rule. A medieval Rabbinic commentator offers an interesting
explanation for this apparent misuse of the word *sh'neiyim:*

5) Cf. Baba Batra, 99a, comment on, "And their faces were turned
   toward the House of God." II Chronicles, 3:13.
6) e.g. *shnay luchot,* "two tablets," Exodus 31:18; *shnay kevasim,*
   "two lambs," Numbers, 28:9, and frequently.

"When you find the word *shnay*, it usually signifies that both things or articles referred to, *hayu shavim b'mareh uv'komah*, are exactly the same in appearance and in size. But when the word *shneiyim* is used (as in our text), it generally signifies *she'en shavim*, that the two things referred to are not equal or the same either in appearance or in size." And to justify his explanation, he quotes an ancient tradition that "one cherub was designed in a masculine image and the second cherub in a feminine image"; and because they were not identical in appearance, the Bible here uses the term *sh'-neiyim*.[7]

What deep insight is revealed in this Rabbinic interpretation of our text! We frequently turn our faces toward the faces of those who are *shavim*, akin to us, either of the same family, or of the same religious group, or of the same race, color, or nationality. But, alas, if *enam shavim*, if they are not the same, if they differ from us in religion, in race, or in color, our faces, even though they may be turned heavenwards while in our sanctuaries, are nevertheless turned away from them and we refuse to regard them as brothers.

There is still another message which we can derive from our text. Note that the two cherubim are not to be placed close to each other. On the contrary: "And make one cherub at the one end and one cherub at the other end . . . thou shalt make the cherubim at its two ends."[8] Though the cherubim are far removed from one another, on opposite ends of the ark-cover, nevertheless, their faces are to be turned each toward its brother.

Again, what a meaningful lesson these Biblical words reveal! We are apt to turn our faces toward those whom we regard as brothers if they are close to us, in the same community, the same city, or the same country. But our text emphasizes that even though we are far removed from our fellow men, even

7) Bachya ibn Pakuda, quoted in Torah Shelemah to Exodus, 25:18, note 129. Cf. Yoma, 62b; Baba Batra, 99a, Rashi, end of page.
8) Exodus, 25:19.

though they may be in another country, aye, even at the other end of the world, we must still look upon them as brothers. The text repeats: *mishne ktzot hakaporet*, "from the two ends of the ark-cover shalt thou make the two cherubim." What hatred, what strife, what wars would be avoided if people of all nations were to learn this Divine truth which the Bible so vividly reveals to us, and which Judaism emphasizes.

And our text conveys a still further, important thought. "How does one portray the figure of a cherub?" the Rabbis ask. "What was the image of the cherubim on the ark-cover?" And they offer a significant answer to their own question: *Dmut partzuf tinok lahem*, "They bore the image of a young child."[9]

What discernment is shown in this interpretation of our Biblical text, and how important it is for us to take this revelation to heart if the ideal of human brotherhood is ever to be realized. We must begin with the young child, implanting within his young mind and heart the lessons of true religion which our text conveys. The world tragedy is due, in large measure, to the circumstance that we teach the young child, by precept and, above all, by example, the very opposite of what our text wishes us to learn. When we teach young children, even in religious schools, so-called facts which are misinterpreted from the Bible, which will fill their hearts with prejudice and hatred toward persons of another religious group, we cannot hope that they will ever espouse the cause of human brotherhood. From their very infancy, as symbolized in the infant form of the cherubim, people must be taught to turn their faces toward their brethren no matter how they may differ in race, color, nationality or religion.

The Biblical text concludes with a message that goes to the heart of what true religion should mean to us: "And there I will meet with thee, and will speak with thee from above the

9) Rashi to Exodus 25:18; cf. Baba Batra, 99a; Chagigah, 13b.

ark-cover, from between the two cherubim."[10] God — and Religion which should represent His voice — speaks to us first and foremost "from between the two cherubim." It is only when we learn the lessons which the cherubim convey that we can truly say that we meet God and that God meets with us.

It is the glory of Judaism that it has always endeavored to emphasize this message as the fundamental lesson of religion. There is a fascinating incident which Rabbi Katina relates in the Talmud: "When the Israelites from all parts of the land went up to the Temple in Jerusalem, on the three festive pilgrimages, those in charge of the Temple would bring out the veil that covered the ark, would unfold it before the incoming pilgrims, and, pointing to the cherubim engraved upon it, would say to them: 'Behold, this exemplifies your love for God!' "[11] The lessons which the cherubim reveal are the first steps which one must take to prove his love for God.

A large part of the world has spurned this message, mocking those who would teach it. They could not or would not understand or appreciate it. In the same passage of the Talmud another sage, Resh Lakish, adds a scene to this tale: "When the heathens entered the Holy Temple and saw the ark-cover, with its cherubim, they tore it from the ark, carried it out to show to their heathen comrades, and mockingly said: 'See, with such things do the Israelites occupy themselves,' and they despised the Israelites."[12]

Yea, the heathen nations and people could mock these truths; but Judaism continued to preach them and Jews continued to uphold them, confident in the faith that the day would come when all men, like the cherubim on the ark-cover, would turn their faces toward the faces of their fellow men and look upon all as brothers, all children of One God, Father of us all.

10) Exodus, 25:22.
11) Yoma, 54a.
12) *Ibid.*, 54b.

For the Sin Which We Have Committed

Preached on eve of Yom Kippur,
October 6, 1954.

In an illuminating address delivered at a recent convention of the Rabbinical Assembly of America, the eminent Jewish philosopher, Professor Abraham Joshua Heschel, bemoaned the fact that modern man — and, speaking to fellow Jews, he referred particularly to the modern Jew — has lost the art of prayer. In a pessimistic note he asked: "Has the synagogue become the graveyard where prayer is buried? Are we, the spiritual leaders of American Jewry, members of a *chevrah kaddisha* (a burial society)?"[1]

It is a good question to put to ourselves, especially on Yom Kippur. This is the one day in the year when the need for prayer should overpower us. It is the singular time when we should feel closest to God, when we should want to lay bare our hearts, through the words uttered with our lips, before our Maker. Professor Heschel continued: "The problem is not one of synagogue *attendance*, but one of *spiritual attendance*." He tried to analyze the causes of this loss of the art of prayer. One of the reasons, he finds, is that we do not trouble ourselves "to study the inner life of the words that fill the world of our prayerbook. . . . It is not enough to know how to translate Hebrew into English . . . a word has a soul, and we must learn how to attain insight into its life. . . . Prayer is not an act of emo-

1) A. J. Heschel, "The Spirit of Jewish Prayer," in *Proceedings of the Rabbinical Assembly of America*, 1953, p. 151 ff. Reprinted in his volume *Man's Quest for God*. (N.Y. 1954), ch. 3.

tion, but rather a way of understanding; it is to religion what thinking is to philosophy."

In the spirit of Professor Heschel's conception, I wish to analyze and to interpret for you one of the most essential prayers we recite on this solemn day, the *Al Chet*, our confession of sins before the Almighty. It is a long list of sins that we enumerate, in couplets for each letter of the Hebrew alphabet. So cardinal is this prayer, that it is said once on the eve of Yom Kippur and repeated three times throughout the morning and afternoon services. It is interesting to note, at the outset, that all of the sins enumerated are of an ethical nature, not one refers to failure in ritual or ceremonial observance. Here is the uniqueness of Judaism, its emphasis on the ethical values of life.

I have often been asked by worshipers in the congregation, "Why must I confess to this long list of sins? I am confident that I have not committed many of them; in fact, I doubt whether anyone, with rarest exception, is guilty of all the sins listed in this confession!" But here is what Professor Heschel must have meant when he spoke of "the inner life," the "soul" of the words. The text of the prayer does not say, *al chet she-chatati*, "for the sin which I have committed," but *al chet she-chatanu*, "for the sin which *we* have committed." In this conscious expression of the word "*we*" is the soul of this prayer revealed. Its emphasis is on social responsibility, a lesson which modern society has not yet fully learned. It is not only the sins which I personally or individually have committed for which I must atone, but also the sins and crimes of others in our society. I bear a responsibility for many of the sinful actions of others as well as for my own. If a murder has been committed in the community I must ask myself whether I have done all that I could have done to help eradicate the social conditions which breed murder and violence. And if I have failed to do my duty, then I, too, bear a share of the guilt for the crime of murder and I must plead for Divine forgiveness.

There is an interesting law in the Bible which goes to the heart of this truth. If a corpse is found lying on the roadside and we do not know who is responsible for the death, then the elders, or leaders, of the nearest community are to be summoned to that spot, "And they shall speak and say: 'Our hands have not shed this blood, neither have our eyes seen it'."[2] The Rabbis, commenting upon this law, ask in surprise: "Do we for a moment suspect that these elders are the perpetrators of the crime?" Their answer is a wise one. "Certainly not! But if this man came to their community hungry and asked for bread to eat, and his plea was unheeded, or if he asked for shelter and was denied, and if he died as a result of this neglect, then the hands of these elders and all their community have shed his blood and bear responsibility for his death."[3]

A new meaning is thus revealed in the few words, "For the sins which *we* have committed!" To neglect our social responsibilities, to fail in our duty to help enact laws and make provisions that could eliminate the evil conditions that breed crimes, makes us co-perpetrators of these very crimes, and we have to seek atonement for our derelictions.

I must quote a further illustration given by the Rabbis to emphasize this truth. They relate that when Rav Assi, one of the great sages of his day, was on his deathbed, his pupils found him weeping. "Rabbi, why do you weep?" they asked. "You who have spent your days studying Torah, you who have given so much charity and performed so many acts of loving kindness, are you afraid to meet your Maker?" "Ah, for this I weep," the sage replied, "that I may have to give an accounting for what I could have done to help enact laws for my people, and which I failed to do!"[4] Here is expressed the genius of the

2) Deuteronomy, 21:1-7.
3) Sotah, 38b, 45b.
4) Tanchuma, Mishpatim, 2.

Jewish religion, that it is our duty to work for the improvement of the social, economic, cultural, and spiritual life of all men by participating in every endeavor necessary to bring about higher standards and conditions of life. "If a man confines himself to a corner in his home," add the Rabbis in this same passage, "and says: '*Mah li b'torach hatzibur*, What concern are the troubles of the community to me? *Mah li bdinehem*, What have I to do with their laws? *Shalom olayik nafshi*, Let me be in peace,' such a man *machriv et haolam*, destroys the world!"[5] Yea, *al chet shechatanu*, "for the sins which *we* have committed" — all of us have need for this confession!

But there is something more which this prayer reveals. Its list of sins to be recited is long and includes some which may be regarded as trivial and others which constitute the most serious transgressions. Why mention all of them in detail? Here, again, let us look at the soul, the inner life of this prayer. What the formulators of this prayer had in mind was simply this, we dare not concentrate on merely one or a few sins, disregarding all the other sins and evils that plague our society. There are many, very many, sins which afflict our social and national life, and we must not make the tragic mistake of focusing all our attention on one sin alone, be it ever so grievous, and of neglecting our other failings and sins.

If I may be permitted to turn to modern events in our national life, we have, alas, a striking example of a failure to understand the truth emphasized by this ancient prayer. The American people, for the last few years,[6] have centered all their thoughts, all their concerns, on one sin, the sin of Communist belief or adherence. I do not wish to be misunderstood; I, too, realize that Communism, especially as exemplified by the rulers of Soviet Russia, is a deadly sin. I know that it is a *chet* which requires our serious attention. But you do not fight that

5) *Ibid.*
6) These words although spoken during the heyday of the Senator McCarthy era, are, alas, in large measure still applicable.

sin by concentrating your entire effort on it alone, by closing
your eyes to all other sins that affect our national life. That is
exactly what the Communists would want us to do. The more
we neglect other wrongs, the more opportunity they have in
their propaganda directed to the hungry and suffering masses
in Asia and in Africa to point to these as failures in the democracies. Although we have disagreed with Arnold J. Toynbee
about his view of Jews and Judaism, that historian is correct
when he states: "The fact that our adversary threatens us by
showing up our defections . . . is proof that the challenge he
presents to us comes not from him, but from ourselves."[7]

It is this exclusive concentration on the one sin, as if it were
the only sin in the world, that has blinded so many of us in
our approach to the entire problem of Communism and pre-
vented us from seeing how we might most effectively weaken
its power and its influence. A keen student of national diplomacy recently made this striking observation: "The bulk of
the planet's population is in the position of a sick man visited
by two doctors. One doctor offers him a pill, a Red one, which
he claims can cure him. The other doctor is looking, not at the
dying man, but at his rival, and is shouting: 'Don't trust that
man! He is a quack!' These exclamations do not constitute a
medical prescription. Which doctor is the dying man likely to
choose?"[8]

Yea, there is a whole list of sins which require our confession. After each section of the prayer we are bidden to repeat
the words: *v'al kulam*, "And for *all* of these sins, O God of
forgiveness, forgive us, pardon us, grant us atonememt." This
is the message that the prayer brings to us and which we must
take to heart if there is to be any hope for man and the world.

And, finally, there is another thought that this important
prayer emphasizes. Each sentence specifying a sin begins with

7) A. J. Toynbee, *Civilization on Trial*, (N.Y. 1948), p. 159.
8) G. F. Hudson, "Point Fourism Is Not Enough," quoting String-
fellow Barr, *Commentary*, (April 1953).

the words: *al chet*, "for the sin." We have many words in Hebrew to denote sin or transgression: *chet* is one of them; *pesha* is another; *avon* is still another. True, there are semantic distinctions among these terms, *chet* is usually translated "sin"; *pesha*, "transgression"; *avon*, "iniquity." The question arises, why does the author of this prayer use the term *chet*, exclusively and not either of the others? May there not have been some psychological reason for the choice of this expression? Here, again, we must follow Professor Heschel's advice and try to penetrate the soul, the inner life, of the words of the prayer.

In the developed usage of the Hebrew language, all these terms have become virtually synonomous. In the beginning, however, there evidently was a pronounced distinction among them. The word *chet*, in its original meaning, implied the idea of "missing the mark." Thus, in one of the earliest books of the Bible, we read of seven-hundred chosen men, who were left-handed, "everyone could sling stones at a hairbreadth, *vlo yachati*, and not miss,"[9] the verb of the same root in *chet*. It is in this original meaning of the term that we may understand why all of us can, in all sincerity, recite this confession.

For have we not all missed the mark toward which we should aim in the virtues or ideals of life? Take, for instance, the confession for the sin of not honoring parents. Even those of us who are not guilty of having actually dishonored them, have we not missed the mark of truly honoring them according to the high demands of our religion? Or, take the sin committed by our lips. Even if we have not lied or spoken falsely, have we not missed the high mark of not uttering a word of gossip detrimental to a neighbor? Even when we respond to appeals for charity, is our gift always compatible with the amount that we should have contributed, or is our offering merely a minimum amount to allay our conscience and to avert the disfavor of the community? Go through the entire list, and see wheth-

9) Judges, 20:16.

er you have not missed the mark of perfection in each area covered by a sin and whether you do not need to seek atonement for these failures! Commenting on the Biblical verse, "Unto Thee, O Lord, belongeth righteousness, but unto us is shame of face,"[10] the Rabbis ask: "What does this mean?" And they answer, in the name of Rabbi Nehemiah: "Even when we do what is righteous or charitable, and then examine our deed, we should indeed be shamefaced."[11]

Our ancestors were very sensitive about failing to reach perfection, even in the apparent absence of sin, and would say in their prayers on this solemn day: "We are not so presumptuous as to say to Thee: We are righteous, *vlo chatanu*, and have not sinned; yea, we have sinned, in having missed the mark of perfection!"

Here, then, is the inner life, the soul, of this ancient prayer of Confession: *Al chet shechatanu*, "For the sin which *we* have committed," all of us sharing in the guilt of the community; *V'al kulam*, "For *all* of the sins," there are many sins and all of them require our serious attention and concern; *V'al chet*, "For the sin of missing the mark of perfection" for such sin, too, we must seek atonement. If we learn to confess to all that the spirit of this prayer implies, then indeed will God's promise for this day be realized: "For on this day shall atonement be made for you, to cleanse you; from all your sins shall ye be clean before the Lord."[12]

10) Daniel, 9:7.
11) Exodus Rabbah, 41:1.
12) Leviticus, 16:30.

Life's
Holiest Purpose

Preached on the eve of Yom Kippur
September 25, 1955.

In the very inspiring prayer which the Jew recites on Rosh Hashanah, the *Unesan'e Tokef*, a prayer which has captivated the
Jewish heart and which forms one of the high motifs of our
liturgy, the author, Rabbi Amnon, who was about to die as a
martyr to his faith, pictures these solemn days as the days of
judgment when "Thou causeth to pass before Thee all human
beings, *kivne maron*, as a flock of sheep." This is the usual
translation of the two Hebrew words that is given in almost every prayer book. This statement was not original with Rabbi
Amnon, it is a quotation from the Mishnah, the earliest code
in the Talmud, where we read that "on Rosh Hashanah all
human beings pass before Him *kivne maron*."[1]

The Rabbis discussing this phrase in the Talmud, were evidently not sure of the exact meaning of this striking phrase,
for they ask: *Mai kivne maron*, "What is meant by the words
kivne maron?"[2] Three Rabbis give us their explanations; and
their answers are not only interesting but also have a special
meaning for us even today. One Rabbi says *kivne imarna*,
"like a flock of sheep."[3] A second, Resh Lakish, says that
the words must be understood to mean: *k'maalot bet maron*,
"like the ascent of Bet Maron." It seems there was such a
steep and narrow path of steps at a place called Bet Maron that

1) Rosh Hashanah, 1:2.
2) *Ibid.*, 18a.
3) Rashi, ibid.

39

wayfarers had to proceed in single file.[4] A third sage, Rav Ye-hudah, deriving the word *maron* from a root which also means soldiers or troops, interprets the phrase to mean: *k'chayalot shel bet David*, "like the soldiers of the House of David."

We have in this discussion not just three different explanations of a Talmudic phrase, but a succinct description of three different ways of life, three portrayals of the behavior of men and women all of whom must pass in judgment before the giver of life and their own conscience. On this day we all pass in review, as it were, and are subject to self scrutiny, the self criticism represented in the words of our daily liturgy: *meh chayenu, mah zidkatenu*, "What is our life, what is its justification?" This precious gift which has been entrusted to us — life — what are we doing with it? And in this phrase of our prayer the Rabbis see us in three categories.

Under one interpretation we appear as the sheep in the field, without thought, without feeling for others, without sympathy, without planning, without ideals or aspirations. Like sheep, we eat, drink, sleep, grind away time, not really living at all, *kivne imarna*. The poet E. E. Cummings aptly describes such persons as "undead" — not living.

Let us be honest with ourselves; let us try to see ourselves as God sees us — our real selves — and tell me, pray, whether this simple description does not accurately portray the so-called life of many of us. The world and all its majestic beauty, with its potential blessedness for all humankind, evokes no response in the soul or mind of those who, like the sheep, have no understanding of what life truly means, whose heart in the words of Mark Twain, is "merely a pump without any other function."[5]

Thus, as we listen to the beautiful strains of these words, "Thou causeth to pass before Thee all human beings, *kivne*

---

4) *idem.*
5) Quoted by Henry Van Wyck Brooks in *Scenes and Portraits*, (N.Y. 1954), p. 15.

maron," let each one ask himself: am I in the category of that Rabbi's interpretation, *kivne imarna?* And if the answer is in the affirmative, then let this day mark the beginning of a new understanding and a new appreciation of what life means and what life demands of us.

In the second interpretation of our text, that given by the sage Resh Lakish, the portrait is drawn of another group of men and women whose lives are *k'maalot bet maron*, "like the ascent of Bet Maron." They have lifted themselves from the likeness of sheep. They have gone upwards; they have ascended the steps of progress. They have advanced in learning, in culture, in knowledge; they have developed in mind; they have acquired an appreciation of the beauties of nature and art. But, alas, in making this ascent, they went alone. Like the wayfarer proceeding in single file along the narrow steps of *Bet Maron*, so too, have many ascended the steps of life alone, with no one at their side. An extreme selfishness fills their whole being. Satisfied with their own ascent in life, they give no thought to and are unconcerned with their fellow men, many of whom may be helpless in the battles of life. These lone climbers march upward, but on the narrow, limited steps sufficient for themselves.

This is the great sin of so many of us for which we must seek forgiveness on this day of judgment, the failure to understand that life is not the true life unless lived with a thought for others. The test of the worthwhile life is the breadth and width of its involvement with our fellow men. The man who takes the upward path with his family at his side has attained a higher level than the one who has proceeded only with his own ambition in mind. The man who ascends with the thought of his community and his people at his side as well has advanced still further. And the man who ascends with the ideal of all humanity at his side has achieved a still higher ascent.

One of the fundamental causes of our world tragedy is this failure to understand what Judaism constantly emphasizes, the social implication of life. This failure is evidenced in every

avenue of life, in the economic, the social, and the political
spheres. We are intended to appraise our lives not by our culture nor by our wealth nor by what heights of progress we have
attained alone, but by the companions of our ascent, — whether our fellow man has been at our side and we at his side.

There is yet a third interpretation of our text, offered by
Rabbi Yehudah: "We pass before Thee, *k'chayalot shel bet
David*, like the soldiers of the House of David." Not just soldiers of an ordinary army, but soldiers battling under the banner of King David! This is a very interesting expression. In
the Jewish tradition, the Messiah was to be a scion of King
David. "Soldiers of the House of David" is a poetic expression for those who battle in behalf of the Messiah, to hasten
the dawn of the Messianic era on earth, soldiers of the Messiah, battling to bring about a new world, a better world for all
mankind.

Noble as it may be to march forward in life with others at
our side, it is also insufficient. We must be soldiers of the
Messiah, seeking to improve the world, to transform the world
with its injustices and inequities into a world of moral order,
a world that will betoken the approach of *malkut shamayim*,
God's kingdom on earth. Here is the supreme test of living —
have we enlisted in the *chayalot shel bet David*, the army of
the House of David? To pass this test, we must work, strive,
battle, sacrifice in order to usher in the Messianic age, when
justice and righteousness will flow like a mighty stream, when
wars will cease, when economic, social, and political justice will
reign, when all men will look upon each other as brothers, children of the living God, Father of us all. This, in substance,
is life's holiest purpose.

Today, we all pass before the throne of God's justice *kivne
maron*. Our life is placed on the scales and weighed. What is it?
What does it stand for? What does it mean? But today we are
also given an opportunity for change, for improvement. We
can begin anew, we can refashion our lives and become a *briah*

chadashah, a new human being.[6] If our lives have been nothing more than the existence of sheep, let us endeavor to change them into something worthwhile, something meaningful and purposeful. If, in our pursuit of higher goals, we have thus far walked alone, let us stretch out our hands and our hearts to embrace our families, our friends, our fellow men so that we may make the ascent of life together. If, thus far, we have been content with the world as it is, let us begin to serve under the banner of the hosts of David to fashion a world as God desired it to be, as God desired us to do.

This is the challenge of this solemn season. May that challenge find a responsive answer in our hearts and thus win for us the life that shall find favor in the sight of God and man.

6) Cf. Midrash to Psalms, 102 end; Leviticus Rabbah, 30:3.

The Psychology of
Prejudice

Preached Sabbath morning,
December 10, 1960.

A most fascinating tale in the Bible is the dramatic story
of Joseph and his brothers. Hall Caine once called it the greatest story in world literature. Thomas Mann, as you recall, made
it the theme of one of his greatest and most popular novels.

The Biblical narrative is of value not only as a work of literature but also as a revelation of the psychological forces working in the mind of man that make for prejudice, prejudice
which turns into hatred and which in its turn causes so much
misery and suffering in the world, to this very day.

There are, of course, many types of prejudice. We have our
prejudices in taste, in customs, in politics, in music and in art,
to name but a few. These are common failings. In most cases
such prejudices are the result of mental immaturity and are
harmless. They can be overcome or corrected, as Professor
Overstreet, in his *Mature Mind*, assures us, by the process of
education.

There is, however, a more harmful form of prejudice, a prejudice towards people of another race, religion, or nationality.
It is to this kind of prejudice that I should like to direct my
discourse. What is the psychological basis of such prejudice?
Scientists, psychologists in particular, offer many scholarly
theories to explain the origin and the prevalence of this malady of prejudice. While some of these are probably valid in
their way, I believe that we have in our Biblical tale of Joseph,

44

a very simple psychological analysis that goes more directly
to the heart of the problem.

You are familiar with the plot of this story. Joseph's father,
Jacob, loved him dearly and presented him with a many-col-
ored coat which aroused his brothers' jealousy and hatred toward him. This hatred was intensified when Joseph related to
them two dreams which he had had.

And then a dramatic scene is portrayed: His brothers go to
feed their father's flock in Shekem; and Jacob summons
Joseph and says to him: "Go now and see whether it is well
with thy brethren." Joseph fulfills his father's request and goes
to Shekem, but fails to see his brothers. "And a certain man
found him, and, behold, he was wandering in the field. And the
man asked him: 'What seekest thou?' And he said, 'I seek my
brethren'.... And the man said, 'They have departed from
here, for I heard them say: "Let us go to Dothan."' And
Joseph went after his brethren, and found them in Dothan.
And they saw him from afar off, and before he came near unto
them, they conspired against him to slay him."[1]

Let us see how the Rabbis read this story, and we shall mar-
vel how their understanding of it helps us to delve into the
deeper aspects of prejudice. "And the man said to Joseph
(this man, according to the Rabbis, was in reality the angel
Gabriel[2]): '*Nasu mizeh*, they have departed from here.'" Any
student of Hebrew can instantly see that the word *mizeh* is
misused. The Hebrew word for *from here* is *mipoh*, not *mizeh*
which literally means *from this*. The Rabbis were surprised at
this apparent mistake in language. But they had a ready answer: "What the man really said to Joseph was: '*Hesiu et atz-
man min ha-achavah*, they have wandered from *this*, the feeling of brotherliness!'"[3] Joseph, in speaking to the stranger,

1) Genesis, 37:3-18.
2) Tanchuma, Vayeshev, 2; Rashi, *ibid.*
3) Rashi to Genesis, 37:17

says: "I seek my brothers"; but the man, or angel in disguise, replies: "They have wandered away from this very idea that you express, the idea of brotherliness!"[4]

Here is the fundamental psychological reason for man's prejudice towards his fellow man: he has departed from the elementary feeling which should fill his heart and mind, the feeling of brotherliness, and thus has lost the sentiment which should guide him in all his relationships with his fellow man. Had man developed this feeling of human brotherliness, and the demands made by such a feeling, he would be incapable of harboring prejudice or hatred toward any fellow being.

See how the story further supports this analysis. "And they saw him *merachok*, from afar off, from the distance, and they conspired to slay him." Ah, here again we discover a basis of prejudice. We look at our fellow man *from the distance*; we do not endeavor to get close to him, to know what he really is, to understand him and what he represents; and because we see him *merachok*, only from afar, we prejudge him, and this is the basis of much of our prejudice. Was there not a great writer who once said about someone he hated: "I do not want to meet him, lest I get to know him and lose my hatred for him!" Yea, looking at our fellow man from afar, without the desire or the effort to get close to him and thus to know him, that is the curse that breeds the disease of prejudice.

And the Rabbis proceed to dissect this disease and what follows from it once we are subject to it. "And the man said to him: 'They have departed from here, for I heard them say: "Let us go to *Dothan*." ' " The story continues: "And Joseph went after his brothers and found them in *Dothan*."

The Rabbis add an extremely interesting observation to this statement when they say perplexedly: "We have searched and searched but could not find in all Canaan a place called *Dothan*." What is the answer to this geographical mystery?

4) Torah Shelemah, to *ib.* 37:17, note 121.

But it is no mystery at all when we understand the Rabbinical explanation. The word evidently does not refer to a place at all. It is derived from the root *dat*, which means religion, or law. The Rabbis tell us that the brothers "went to seek *nikle datot*, religious or legal reasoning, with which to rationalize their prejudice and to justify their desire to slay him."[5] Yea, here is the crux of the problem. First we become contaminated with the germ of prejudice, and then we seek reasons and arguments with which to justify our prejudice. This too-often successful effort to rationalize our unjustifiable prejudices and hatreds is what makes it so difficult to eradicate them.

Take anti-Semitism as one example. There recently appeared a volume, *Essays on Anti-Semitism*, edited by Koppel S. Pinson, and written by various scientists and men of letters. Professor Israel Wechsler, an eminent neurologist and psychologist, discussing the "Psychology of Neurotics," writes: "The attempt has been made to explain anti-Semitism on religious grounds, economic grounds, on physical racial grounds; but it becomes clear even on a superficial analysis that many of the reasons given are no reasons at all. . . . The phenomenon of anti-Semitism becomes understandable as we realize that culture and civilization are but thin veneers, and that the human animal is still considerably blind and emotional in his behavior." This is the truth about all forms of prejudice towards anyone of a different color, religion, race or nationality. Our reasons are no reasons at all. They are the *nikle datot*, the crude and often crafty rationalizations which we adopt later in an effort to justify our actions, and which make it so difficult to eradicate this disease from the hearts and minds of many men and women.

But our story penetrates still deeper in its analysis of the subject. "They hated him and they could not speak peaceably

5) Rashi to Genesis, 37:17; Torah Shelemah, *ibid.*, note 121 for various versions and references.

unto him."[6] That is the usual translation found in the English versions. No translation, however, can truly reveal the deeper meaning of an original text; thus the Hebrew text tells us much more. "And they could not speak *l'shalom*, peaceably unto him." The word *l'shalom*, literally, does not mean *peaceably*; in Hebrew it is *b'shalom* that means *in peace*, or *peaceably*. *L'shalom*, literally means for *peace*; and what our text seeks to convey is that "they could not speak *for peace* unto him."[7] That is the tragedy which usually results from the affliction of prejudice. We cannot speak *for* peace, or, as the Aramaic translation has it, *lo tzavan*, "they did not *want* to talk for peace."[8] It was not that they *could not*, but that they *did not want* to discuss even the possibility of achieving peace between them. Prejudice, and the hatreds that it produces, are so deep-rooted that the individual resists every influence that may cleanse his heart and mind and lead him to live in peace instead of hate with his fellow man.

The Hebrew text elaborates upon this phase of our theme. The Hebrew word *dabro* does not literally mean what the English version says: "They could not *dabro*, speak." *Dabro* means *his speaking*. What the text wishes to emphasize is that his brothers "could not stand *dabro*, his speaking for peace." Joseph wanted to talk peace with them: "I seek my brethren," he says. "He came *vsho'el bishlomam*, and asked for their peace, *v'lo hayu moshivim oto*, but they did not even answer him."[9] Even if the aggrieved tries to speak peace and to plead *l'shalom*, for peace, his plea often remains unheeded because of deep-rooted prejudice. This is true not only in the case of individuals but also in the case of nations and governments. How many of our current nationalistic hatreds, so often the result of prejudice, could and would disappear if the na-

6) *Ibid.*, v. 4.
7) *Cf.* Ibn Ezra to this verse.
8) Targum Onkelos, to Genesis, *ibid.*
9) Torah Shelemah, to Genesis, 37:4, note 56.

tions wanted to talk peace and to discuss ways to achieve peace!

Here, then, we have Judaism's analysis, suggested by the Bible and its Rabbinic interpreters, of the disease of prejudice, an analysis which goes more tellingly into the heart of the problem than many of our modern scientific treatments of the subject.

"All that happened to Joseph," the Rabbis tell us, "happened to Zion"[10]—and to the Jew whom Zion here symbolizes. The Jew is the classic, though, alas, not the sole, example of the target of this prejudice of the world in all the aspects of our interpretation. He endeavored to develop, and his prophets and sages continuously encouraged him to develop, the feeling of brotherliness toward his fellow man; and to this day pleads with them *l'shalom* for mutual peace. Alas, as in the case of Joseph's brothers, many refuse even to answer his plea. The attitude of the Arab states to Israel of today is an illustration of this sad truth.

Here is the role that Judaism asks religion to assume: to keep emphasizing the deeper meaning of the story of Joseph and his brothers — until each man takes it to heart and says: "I seek the peace and the welfare of my fellow man, my brother!"

---

10) Tanchuma, Vayigash, 10.

Conquering the Heavens, and Losing the Earth

Preached on Rosh Hashanah,
September 29, 1962.

We are still under the magic spell of the remarkable achievements recently witnessed in man's conquest of space: the orbiting of the earth, not just once but many times, by our American and by the Russian cosmonauts. These feats stagger our imagination. Man has indeed become, to use a Rabbinic phrase, *shutaf l'ha-kadosh baruch Hu*, "a co-worker with the Holy One, blessed be He, in the process of creation."[1] Man is fashioning the vistas of new worlds.

At this very moment, the American Mariner is racing through space toward the planet Venus; and we have lately been assured by the President of the United States that within a decade an American spaceman will land on the moon. A new age has dawned, the Space Age, in which, as President Kennedy stated in his recent address in Houston, Texas, "The eyes of the world now look into space, to the moon and to the planets beyond."

This urge to reach out into space, to go beyond the confines of the earth and to touch the very heavens, is not novel. The methods, of course, are new; the accomplishments are new, but the yearning, the desire, span recorded history. In the early chapters of our Bible we have two tales that illustrate this fact.

You recall first the story of the Tower of Babel. Just a few generations after the great flood, which had destroyed all hu-

---

1) Cf. Shabbat, 10a.

50

man beings with the exception of Noah and his family, the people gathered together and said one to another: "Come, let us build us a city and a tower, whose top reaches to heaven, and let us make for ourselves a name."[2] Everyone concentrated on this single task. "And the whole earth was of one language and the same speech."[3] On with the building of a tower that will reach the heavens! Nothing else concerned them. The Rabbis, amplifying the Biblical account, tell us: "If, in the process of building, a man fell and was killed, no one gave a care, not even a glance on the body of the victim. But if a brick fell, they cried and wept, "Oh, how long it will take to replace it!' "[4] It was a remarkable achievement for those days. The Rabbis say that "the tower was already so high that it took a man a whole year to reach to the top of it."[5] You know, of course, the conclusion of the story. God, accompanied by a host of angels, descended from heaven, confused the people's speech and scattered them to the four corners of the earth. And that was the end of the Tower of Babel an edifice built to reach heaven.

Several chapters later, we read of another incident. The patriarch Jacob, fleeing from the wrath of his brother Esau, is sleeping upon a bed of rocks. "And he dreamed, and behold a ladder set upon the earth, and the top of it reached high heaven; and the angels of God were ascending and descending on it. And behold, the Lord stood on it."[6] Again, reaching out unto the heavens!

Two episodes with a similar content, and yet what a contrast between them! The first arouses God's anger; the second wins God's praise and His promises to Jacob for a bright future,

2) Genesis, 11:4.
3) *Ibid.*, v. 1.
4) Pirke d'R. Eliezer, 24; Torah Shelemah, Genesis, 11:4, note 38.
5) *Ibid.* Cf. Louis Ginzberg, *Legends of the Jews*, 5:p. 202, note 88 for added references.
6) Genesis, 12:12,13. The latter phrase is translated according to the view of R. Chiya, Genesis Rabbah, 69:2.

above all, that, "In thee and in thy seed shall all the families of the earth be blessed."[7]

A deeper study of the Hebrew text, and, above all, the Rabbinic comments on that text, will reveal the great distinction inherent in the two incidents.

In the tale of the Tower of Babel, the Rabbis declare that the people said to each other: *naaseh avodah zarah brosho,* "We will set an idol upon the top of the tower, and *nitten cherev b'yadah,* in its hand we will place a sword; *v'naaseh milchamah imo,* we will make war against God, and all that God stands for!"[8] This was their real intent in reaching out to the heavens: to enthrone a new god, the sword, with which to make war against all that the old God had taught, about Whom they said: "We desire neither Him nor His protection!"[9] Nay, their aim went further: "And we will make for ourselves a name";[10] that is, a reputation as the conquerors of God and His world! How familiar this picture now becomes.

Jacob also dreams of reaching out unto the heavens. But, on top of the ladder that touches heaven, he sees God Himself standing, revealed in all His glory. And Jacob sees angels, contrary to what we would imagine, not first descending from the heavens to earth and then ascending back to their heavenly abode, but ascending from the innermost recesses of his mind, heart and soul,[11] up the ladder until they catch a glimpse of God, and then descending, bringing back the Divine inspiration to bless the lives of men here on earth.

What a lesson and what a challenge these two pictures are for our world in this age of space exploration. Judaism is not opposed to these new scientific ventures, nor to research in the

7) Genesis, 28:14.
8) Genesis Rabbah, 38:6. Cf. Sanhedrin, 109a.
9) *Ibid.,* 38:7.
10) Genesis, 11:4.
11) Again, the interpretation is according to R. Chiyah, Genesis Rabbah, 68:18.

realm of space. With the Psalmist, it proclaims: "How great is Thy work, O Lord; Thy thoughts are very deep!"[12] And it is man's privilege to utilize the mind that God gave him, to discover the mysteries of God's works and thoughts. The question that should concern man is: What is the motive that prompts these explorations? Is it to bring life and good to man, or is it to enthrone the sword, to utilize these achievements for death and evil, for wars and destruction?

It is interesting to note that at the government reception tendered in Moscow a few months ago to honor the latest two Russian cosmonauts for their brilliant achievements, the Minister of Defense, in his congratulatory address, boasted: "Now we have an instrument of war that will put fear into the hearts of all who oppose us!" Almost the very words shouted by the people who had built the Tower of Babel, who had wanted to enthrone the sword as their new god, and who had proclaimed: "We will make war against Him and His Law!"

The transformation of a great good into an instrument of evil, that is the tragedy facing the world today! I am now better able to understand a passage in the Bible that, I must confess, has baffled me and has baffled many of the Bible commentators. You recall the story of Adam who had been placed in the Garden of Eden and had been warned by God: "Of every tree of the garden thou mayest freely eat; *ume'etz hadaat tov vara*, but of the tree of the knowledge of good and evil, thou shalt not eat of it; for in the day that thou eatest thereof, thou shalt surely die."[13] We Jews glory in the fact that Judaism has ever encouraged the acquisition of knowledge, that learning and the pursuit of knowledge are the very foundations of our religion. How can we conceive of God's forbidding man to taste of the tree that symbolizes this great gift? Nay, more, the tree of the knowledge of *tov vara*, of good and evil! Is not

12) Psalms, 92:6.
13) Genesis, 2:16, 17.

this the very function of religion, to know the distinction between what is good and what is evil? But look closely at the Hebrew text. It does not say what we thought it meant, at all! The
meaning is *not* what the usual English translation gives us.
Literally, the text says: "And of the tree *hadaat tov vara*, of
the knowledge of good *and* evil," in other words, both at the
same time, that knowledge which turns good into evil, which
transforms good knowledge into an instrument of evil! No
wonder that it was the poisonous serpent that urged Adam
and Eve to taste the fruit of that kind of knowledge!

We want to hope that America is truly prompted by a different motive, one beautifully expressed by President Kennedy
in that Houston address, when he said: "We have vowed that
we shall not see space filled with weapons of mass destruction,
but with instruments of knowledge and understanding." There
would be no sense in America's spending billions of dollars to
reach the moon or to approach the planet Venus if the only
purpose is *naase lanu shem*, "that we make a name for ourselves," that we have an instrument that can be used for evil!
The heavens to which we soar, *mesaprim k'vod el*, "declare the
glory of God,"[14] and these space explorations should inspire us
to embrace a vision of Godliness meant to advance and to
enhance man's life on earth. How sadly we need this vision to
do away with the miseries and horrors that fill the earth today!

A motion picture was recently shown in the neighborhood
theaters. I did not see the film and do not know its story. But
I was fascinated by its title: *The Sky Above, and the Mud Below!* What a striking contrast there is between the Divine glory
that the heavens reveal and the mud, the filth of suffering,
of ignorance, of hate so rampant here below! Let it not be said
of us that we have conquered the heavens but have lost the
earth!

Above all, as the astronauts scan the heavens in their flights

14) Psalms, 19:2.

through space, they see the orderliness, the harmony, the peace that reign in the realms above. To quote again from President Kennedy's address: "There is no strife, no prejudice, no national conflict in outer space, as yet." The Rabbis of old express the same thought even more pointedly. Commenting on the verse, *Oseh shalom bimromav,* "He maketh peace in His realms above,"[15] these sages make a keen observation: "See, in the heavenly spheres there are the clouds of water and the stars of fire, but the water does not quench the fire nor the fire consume the water, *hem darim zeh im zeh,* they abide in harmony one with the other."[16] And we Jews repeat these words of Job three times daily, as we conclude the important *Amidah* prayer, and hopefully add the words: "May He confer that kind of peace upon us!" We mean the peace that can come only when peoples of all races and all faiths, when nations of differing ideologies, will learn from the heavenly hosts to dwell side by side, *darim zeh im zeh* each with its own ways, yet without the desire to annul the ways of others.

Yea, more, these conquests of space should make us realize that just as there are universal physical laws ruling the world, so, too, there are universal moral laws ruling the world. A great Jewish sage and philosopher of the tenth century, Saadya Gaon, made a beautiful observation with reference to this very thought:[17] "The Bible uses the same metaphor, *'finger of God,'* when speaking of the heavenly spheres, 'When I see the heavens the work of *Thy fingers,* the moon and the stars which Thou hast fixed firm,'[18] and also when speaking of the tablets of God's moral law, 'written by the finger of God.' "[19] The Divine creative force that is responsible for the glorious heavens and the

15) Job, 25:12.
16) Yalkut Shimoni, Job, 25:2; Tanchuma, Terumah, 11.
17) Quoted in Torah Shelemah, in Exodus, 8:15, note 50
18) Psalms, 8:4.
19) Exodus, 31:18.

heavenly hosts is also the same force that fashioned the Moral Law to guide the destiny of man.

On this anniversary of the creation of the world let us take pride in man's great conquests in penetrating many of the mysteries of the physical world. But let us now begin to master the moral laws to guide and to rule the lives of men on earth, so that we may live to see the day when not only "the heavens declare the glory of God," but also the earth, and the men of earth, will declare the same glory of God!

The Worship
of the Golden Calf

Preached on Yom Kippur
October 5, 1957.

Most of the Jewish holidays commemorate specific events in our history. Thus, Passover, on the fifteenth of *Nissan*, marks the date when the Israelites were freed from their bondage in Egypt. Shavuot, or Pentecost, observed on the sixth day of *Sivan*, commemorates, according to Jewish tradition, the giving of the Torah on the mountain of Sinai. Hanukkah and Purim are observed on the anniversaries of the events they commemorate. Even *Rosh Hashanah*, our New Year, is associated with certain historic events. It marks the creation of the world. The Rabbis enumerate other historic events occurring on the first day of *Tishre*, which Rosh Hashanah also commemorates.[1] What historic event does *Yom Kippur*, our Day of Atonement, commemorate? True, it is the day of penitence and forgiveness of sins; but why is it observed on this specific date, the tenth day of *Tishre*?

The Rabbis do give an answer, and their answer is most significant. They link this particular day with the incident of the *maase ha-egel*, the making of the golden calf. You recall the incident. Just a short time after the Israelites, standing at the foot of Sinai, had loudly proclaimed: "We will do and we will hearken," and while Moses was still on the mountain top about to deliver the tablets of God's Law, the Israelites suddenly forgot their own words and made for themselves a gold-

---

1) Rosh Hashanah, 11a.

en calf, before which they danced and cried: "These are thy gods, O Israel!"[2] And you remember what followed. Moses came down from the mountain with the tablets in his hands, and when he saw what his people were doing, his countenance drooped in disappointment, and, in anger, he cast the tablets to the ground, shattering them.[3] The Rabbis, adding a fine touch to the Biblical account, tell us that when God saw what Moses had done, He congratulated him and said: *y'yasher kochaka sheshavarta,* "Thou hast done well that thou hast broken them!"[4] The tablets would be useless to a people worshiping a golden calf.

The Bible continues the tale, describing how God wanted to destroy the people for their unfaithfulness, how Moses, the great lover of his people despite their faults, pleaded in their behalf, and how, finally, God yielded to his fervent plea saying: "I have forgiven, according to your words," and gave him the second tablets of the Law. "It was on the tenth day of *Tishre,*" the Rabbis tell us, "when God acquiesced to the plea of Moses, and forgave the people for their sin of worshiping the golden calf; and it was then that God ordained that that date be designated as a day of atonement for all future generations."[5]

Of all the backslidings of which the Israelites were guilty while in the wilderness, this sin was regarded by the Rabbis as one of the gravest, a sin to be remembered and recalled at all future times, the worshiping of the idol of gold. It was the sin that caused the breaking of the *luchot,* the divine tablets of the moral law.

Let us go more deeply into the nature of this sin, which we are to recall on this Day of Atonement. What was the nature of its seriousness? The Rabbis, in their attempt to fathom its

2) Exodus, 32:8.
3) *Ibid.,* v. 19.
4) Shabbat, 87a.
5) Tanchuma, *Ki Tisa,* 31. Cf. Baba Batra, 121a, and Rashi, *ibid.*

deeper meaning, give us a curious explanation. They picture Moses as pleading with God: "Master of the world, it was the gold and silver which Thou hast bestowed upon them in abundance, *ad she'amru dai*, so that they said: 'It is enough,' that was what caused them to make a god of gold."[6]

This statement is usually misunderstood by the average reader who thinks that it refers to the Israelites as saying to God, when He granted them the gold and silver of the Egyptians, "It is enough, give us no more!" That is contrary to what we usually observe in human nature. It is rare that you will find a man laden with gold saying, "I have enough, I want no more!" What Moses really meant was that the Israelites had been so blinded by the gold they now possessed, that they said *dai, this is enough in life*; nothing else is worthwhile; gold alone is the all-sufficiency in life. When people adopt such a life philosophy, it naturally follows that they make a god of their gold, a god who demands complete obeisance, whom they worship above all else, before whom they dance and proclaim: "This is our god!" When this happens, morality is destroyed, ideals lose their potency, culture is of no value, civilization is no more.

The Rabbis, commenting upon the name of a site in the wilderness which the Bible calls *di zahav*,[7] tell us that it was this very site on which the idol of gold had been fashioned,[8] and that it was to bear this name, *di zahav*, "gold alone is enough," for all time to come, to serve as a lasting reminder of that great sin.

If I were to characterize the world in which we live today, I would say it worshiped *di zahav*, "the *all-sufficiency* of gold!" Not in God, but in gold we put our trust! If you want to understand the true meaning of all the man-made tragedies that afflict our world, it is this *di zahav*, which has turned our world

6) Yoma, 86b; Sanhedrin, 102a.
7) Deuteronomy, 1:1.
8) Rashi, *ibid.*; Berakot, 32a.

into a vale of tears and sorrows. One of the Rabbis, analyzing many of the tragedies that have afflicted the world, comes to the conclusion: "There is no punishment, no tragedy that has come to the world that has not within it some measure of the original idol of gold."[9]

It is not that gold in itself is bad or evil. Our sages, in a striking comment, tell us that originally God did not want to create gold, foreseeing the evils and the tragedies that it might bring about. But He also saw that gold could be used for the erection of a holy sanctuary, for good causes, and so He bethought Himself and created it.[10] There is gold that can serve to bless and to enhance the life of man just as there is gold that can be a curse to man. As R. Chisda says: "There are two kinds of gold — *zahav stam v'zahav tov*, — there is gold that is ordinary and there is gold that is good."[11] Gold is evil when it is worshiped, when it becomes our god.

That is at the heart of the world's tragedy. I do not wish to go into a detailed analysis of the political and diplomatic difficulties that face mankind today, the wars and the threats of wars that we behold. The root of most of these evils is the worship of the idol of gold, which makes naught of truth, of justice, of righteousness. This sin affects the whole world. You see it in our system of education. A generation or two ago the student was encouraged to study the classics, Latin and Greek, the thinking of ancient philosophers. Today all this is dismissed. Such study has no practical value, it cannot help in attaining material success. Only studies that lead to the acquisition of gold are encouraged today. You see it in our economic life, the business man who sacrifices everything, his very health, in the worship of this idol, and whose reward is often ulcers, shattered nerves, even a broken life. Our mental hospitals are filled to overflowing and cannot keep pace with

9) Sanhedrin, 102a.
10) Genesis Rabbah, 16:3; Exodus Rabbah, 35:1.
11) Yoma, 44b.

the steady increase of nervous breakdowns, mental deterioration, the result, in many cases, of this intense worship of gold. The corruption revealed among some of the leaders in labor unions and in business management, the violation of ethical and legal standards by some of the heads of great corporations, and even the tremendous increase of juvenile delinquency which now plagues our country, much of this can be traced, directly and indirectly, to the great sin, the worship of the idol of gold.

Recently, a feature article appeared in *The New York Times*, in which the author quotes one of Balzac's characters, the Village Rector, who on his return from a visit to America, described it as "that land of money and selfishness, where souls are cold." And the author also quotes Europeans who refer to America as "the kingdom of the dollar god."[12] True, it ill befits the pot to call the kettle black. These descriptions are as true of European countries and of other peoples today as they are of America. It is the *makat ha-olam*, "the plague which infests the entire world." But that does not excuse us from acknowledging the sin that has overtaken many of the people in our own land. Virtually everyone, and everything, is judged today by the dollar standard, and *di zahav* — the all sufficiency of gold — has become the accepted motto of most of the people in our land. We are a prosperous people and can thank God for it. Our prosperity could be the means of bringing sunshine into many a darkened life. But, as God says in the words of the prophet: "And the silver and gold which I multiplied for her they made into a *baal*, an idol!"[13]

Alas, this sin is affecting our Jewish life as well. We did have, in the past, a measure of values. For instances, the *talmid chakam*, the student, the man of learning and culture, the idealist, was the aristocrat looked up to by all others in the

12) "French Fiction and American Reality", by R. C. Bruckberger, in Book Section, *The New York Times*, (July 31, 1955).
13) Hosea, 2:10.

community. The individual who served his fellow man, who spent his life in *gemilut chasadim*, in the performance of loving kindness, was regarded as the ideal to be emulated by all others. Today, material success has become the idol to which many of us dedicate our lives. In olden times, the infant in the cradle heard the lullaby: *Torah is die beste schoireh*, "Torah, learning, is the best commodity," and the child was inspired to devote his life in its pursuit. Today, cleverness, shrewdness, the tricks of the trade, anything that can help to attain material success, are instilled in the heart of the child. No wonder that young couples today want to start out with the flush of material prosperity which their parents may have achieved only after a lifetime of struggle and hardship. I have seen families which for many years had lived in peace suddenly turned into warring camps, relatives bitterly hating each other, all because of dissatisfaction and disagreement about the division of money bequeathed by a parent. Again, the worship of the idol of gold! Yea, we Jews, too, have become ensnared by the materialistic philosophy of the age. No wonder that God wanted us in every age to recall the incident of the golden calf, to seek forgiveness for this sin of which we too are guilty.

It is interesting to see how the ancient Rabbis, in enacting the regulations with regard to the Day of Atonement, pursue this very thought which I have endeavored to propound to you. On this most solemn of all days in the year, the High Priest was to enter the Holy of Holies to plead for atonement on behalf of his people. He was to adorn himself in the finest and purest of robes on that occasion,[14] *but the robes were not to bear any trimming of gold*. And the sages ask: "Why could not the High Priest adorn himself with garments of gold?" Their answer is most significant. "The prosecutor cannot become the defender. We dare not give Satan the opportunity to say to God: yesterday they made of gold an idol, and today

14) Leviticus, 16:4.

they come before Thee with the very gold to plead forgiveness!"[15] On this holiest of all days we are to cleanse our eyes and purify our minds from the very sight and thought of this gold which we have so unfortunately learned to worship.

The Rabbis also carry this thought through in their interpretation of the laws pertaining to the *shofar*, the horn whose sounds are heard on Rosh Hashanah and at the conclusion of Yom Kippur: "It is not permitted to use a *shofar* that is trimmed with gold at the part which is touched by the human lips, nor a *shofar* that is adorned with gold on the inside. If the sound that it is to produce is affected in the slightest degree by any gold upon it, it is forbidden to make use of it."[16] How clearly and how emphatically they keep emphasizing the danger of making gold an object of man's worship.

And now we should understand why it it is this tenth day of *Tishre* that has been decreed by God as the day on which we should atone for this great sin, on which we should recognize the inherent dangers of a life based on *di zahav*, on the all sufficiency of gold. The great philosopher Santayana, in his autobiographical work,[17] pays tribute to a teacher who taught him "to possess and not to be possessed!" It is this truth which Yom Kippur emphasizes, to possess gold, but not to be possessed by it. May we learn this truth, and God will say to us, as he said to Moses: "I have forgiven according to thy words." We shall then be able to accept anew the tablets of God's Law, which alone can make life meaningful and worthwhile.

15) Rosh Hashanah, 26a; Leviticus Rabbah, 21:9.
16) Rosh Hashanah, 27b.
17) G. Santayana, *Persons and Places*, (N.Y., 1944), Vol. 1.

The Barbarian
in Man

Preached on Rosh Hashanah,
September 11, 1961.

Rosh Hashanah, in Jewish tradition, is the judgment day not only of the Jew but of all mankind. It marks the creation of the world and the world's judgment day. We are the only people who take note of these events. As we say in our prayer service: "This day the world came into being, on this day all human beings stand in judgment!"

As we look upon the world situation today, it is not a very promising scene that we behold. In the words of the prophet we may say: *lo yom v'lo leylah*, "it is not day and it is not night"[1] Fortunately, the darkness of the night has not come upon us; a third world war has still been stayed. But, alas, neither is it day, for the sun does not yet shine. The cold war continues, and wherever we turn we still see fighting and bloodshed, hatred and cruelty. At the least provocation man seizes the gun, ready to shoot and to kill. A prominent American psychologist recently told us: "If this was the best of all possible words, the outlook for man was gloomy indeed." And he comes to the conclusion that "It's getting a little strenuous to stay an optimist."[2]

For a little while things look more hopeful and we begin to think that the light of day is appearing, when suddenly our

1) Zakariah 14:7.
2) Dr. Alfred Farau, addressing the American Association of Adlerian Psychology.

64

hopes are shattered and we are back again in the shadows of darkness. The brilliant French author, Albert Camus, winner of the Nobel Prize, who recently met his tragic death, compares man's passage through the world to the pointless labor of the mythological character, Sisyphus, who had been condemned to roll a giant boulder up a steep hill. Since it would roll back down each time, the man had to repeat the same pointless labor perpetually.[3] This image vividly describes the world situation today.

What is at the root of the pointless and fruitless effort of man which leads nowhere and so particularly marks the present world tragedy? I think the answer lies in a unique phrase in the Bible. You recall the story of Ishmael, about whom we read in the Torah lesson of this festival, and of whom the angel, appearing before his mother Hagar in her distress, said: "And he shall be *pe're adam*, a wild man."[4] There is something strange in that Hebrew expression. In the Hebrew language, unlike most other languages, the adjective follows the noun. In English we say, "a wild man"; *wild*, being the adjective, precedes the noun, *man*. In Hebrew, it should be, according to grammatical rules, the reverse, *adam pe're*. But in our Biblical text, we read *pe're adam*, with the adjective followed by the noun, a most unusual construction in Hebrew.

Evidently, the Bible meant something deeper than the words of the usual English translation. There is no grammatical mistake in our text. *Pe're* is not the adjective here but the noun, and *adam* is the adjective. What the angel really said was: he will be *wildness* in *human form!* Not a human being in essence, though a little wild at times, but wildness masked as a human being. The angel's description, I take it, is not meant solely for Ishmael nor for his descendants, but for the majority of all mankind. Man is still the barbarian — wild-

3) *The Myth of Sisyphus.* (N.Y. 1955).
4) Genesis, 16:12.

ness in essence — though he may dress and, at times, talk like
a human being.

One of the great theologians of our day, speaking of the
all-conquering barbarians who overpowered ancient Rome, aptly says: "The barbarian is not necessarily known by his bear-
skin or his axe. He may be as urbane as the eighteenth-cen-
tury philosopher, who prepared the way for the guillotine and
the tumbrels. Or in one man's words, he may wear a Brooks
Brothers suit and carry a ball-point pen. . . . In fact, even be-
neath the academic gown there may lurk a child of the wilderness."[5]

The Eichmann trial has given us the clearest example of
this *pe're adam*, this wildness in a human mask. As we look at
Adolf Eichmann in his glass cage, he seems to possess all the
signs of a human being. He would be the last man to be chos-
en by a stage director for the role of a villain in a play. He looks
so kind, so gentle, as though he would hesitate to kill even a
fly. But his heart is the heart of the wild savage. It is only the
facade of a human being that you see. In the essence of his
being he is a classic example of the *pe're adam!*

And there are innumerable little Eichmanns in every part
of the world. You see them in the South of our own country.
They appear on our television screens as barbarians, with clubs
in their hands and rage in their eyes, ready to attack a little
girl on her way to school, for no other reason than that God
had created her with a skin that was dark. You hear of them
masquerading in human form, correctly attired, as smooth-
speaking diplomats who, when approached with the Eichmann
offer to exchange a million Jews threatened with the gas cham-
ber for seven thousand trucks, coldly replied: "What would we
do with a million Jews?"

We see evidence of this barbarism in the theses now propounded by some scientists. The one comfort we all thought
we had with regard to our threatened world was the very knowl-

5) Father J. C. Murray, in *We Hold These Truths* (N.Y. 1960).
   Quoted in *Time* Magazine, (December 12, 1960).

edge that nuclear weapons, if used by both the East and the West would destroy all of us, and no one would conquer. We thought that was the great deterrent keeping each side from firing the first shot. Everyone took it for granted that a war under present conditions would be a mutual suicide pact. But now come scientists who, in a desire to free man from this deterrent, and with the callousness of a *pe're adam*, assure us that our fear is groundless, that the future of the world, after such a war, would not be so bleak as we had been led to believe.

One scientist, in a recent book which has attracted wide attention, after discussing the aftermath of such a war, asks in matter-of-fact fashion, "Will the survivors envy the dead?" And he answers: "No! Despite a widespread view to the contrary, objective studies indicate that even though the amount of human tragedy would be greatly increased in the postwar world, the increase would not preclude normal and happy lives for the majority of the survivors and their decendants."[6] And he tries to assure us that within ten years those who survived would be able to rebuild the world. With what blandness he makes this optimistic claim!

Is there then no hope? Is man to remain the essence of wildness in human form? There are many today who emphatically answer "Yes!" Man is a savage and he will remain the *pe're adam*. We will always have wars and bloodshed and cruelties; for man is evil and the world is evil! You see and hear that answer in the mood of pessimism which prevails among many of the enlightened men and women today. It is reflected in the modern philosophies which are propounded; in the Existentialism of a Jean-Paul Sartre, who insists that "Evil is absolute and irredeemable"; in many of the popular plays on our stage, and in much of the literature of our age. The tremendous popularity which the works of the late Ernest Hemingway

6) Herman Kahn, *On Thermonuclear War* (Princeton University Press 1960). See the excellent review of this work by H. Stuart Hughes, entitled "A Strategy of Deterrence" in *Commentary*, (March 1961).

enjoyed is attributed by many literary critics to the ready audience of those responsive to the profound pessimism and sense of doom which they expressed. The hero in his *Farewell To Arms*, says: "I had seen nothing sacred, and the things that were glorious had no glory, and the sacrifices were like the stockyards at Chicago if nothing was done to the meat except to bury it." Again, the big words were false, and life itself "was just a dirty trick," as the dying heroine tells her lover in the same book. In *Death in The Afternoon*, Hemingway states his tragic creed flatly: "There is no remedy for anything in life!"

Is this the judgment which we Jews are taught to accept, that all is hopeless? No! A thousand times no! Judaism sees the evil in man, but proclaims that it can be eradicated, that man has the power to choose between the good and the evil, and needs but the will to make the right choice. Man can transform the *pe're*, the wildness within him, into an *adam*, a human being who reflects the image of the Divine. Life is not a dirty trick, but a challenge to conquer the barbarism within us. That is the message of this judgment day. It calls to us to repent and to change, and it gives us the assurance that man can change.

The process of humanizing man may take a long time, but we dare not give up hope. After all, man is young in the process of his cultural and spiritual development. You recall what the Bible tells us. After the flood in the days of Noah, God promised that never again would He destroy the world, "for the nature of the heart of man is evil *min'urav*."[7] This Hebrew word is usually translated "from his youth." I think the Hebrew text has a deeper and more tenable meaning. The Hebrew letter *m*, preceding a word, means not only *from*, but also *because*. What God really said was that "the nature of the heart of man is evil *because* of his youth!"

7) Genesis, 8:21.

Even according to the historian Toynbee, the emergence of civilized man can be traced to a time only six or seven thousand years ago. And Julian Huxley, in his *Evolution in Action*, (N.Y. 1953), tells us: "To the historical specialist, the five or six thousand years of civilization seems intolerably long. But this is a minute interval to the biologist. Man is very young; the human deployment is in an explosive and very early phase. . . . He is not an animal; he is something new in evolution, and he has a boundless future. . . . Man has an unlimited field of possibilities." We must be patient and work towards man's perfection. Man has progressed in his knowledge; he is conquering space and will eventually make his way to the planets. But as General De Gaulle recently remarked: "We may well go to the moon, but that is not very far. The greatest distance we have to cover still lies within us!" That distance can be overcome if we but have the will. As the Rabbis tell us: "It is not for you to complete the task, but neither are you free to desist from it."[8]

Let us, each of us, resolve on this solemn day to make a new beginning, first of all to transform our own lives to rid ourselves of the wildness that is still within each of us, and then to strive for the transformation of the world. Let each one dedicate his life to work for peace and social justice, for righteousness and human brotherhood, and thus free man's heart from the barbarism which now lurks therein. The boulder of man's hopes and prayers will then be pushed higher and higher up the mountain of true progress, without fear of its rolling downward, until all mankind embraces and follows the rule of God, the source of all happiness.

8) Abot, 2:21

The Two Trumpets
of World Redemption

Preached on Rosh Hashanah,
October 1, 1951.

We come on this judgment day of the world and lay bare our hearts before our Maker, seeking guidance and inspiration for the battles of life that confront us. We find ourselves today at, what I would call, the crossroads of history. We face two paths, one that could lead to world peace and happiness, the other to human destruction and annihilation. If only we knew which to choose!

Let us see whether *Rosh Hashanah* can help us to find and to choose the path which leads to life for us and for all mankind. Perhaps the Jewish tradition has a message which can guide the Jew and the world in these days of vital decision.

This holy day is associated in the Jewish mind with the dramatic Biblical story which tells of Abraham's readiness to sacrifice his only son, Isaac, in obedience to God's request.[1] We read this tale as the Biblical portion assigned for *Rosh Hashanah*. The *Shofar*, or ram's horn, is sounded on this solemn festival to remind us of this momentous incident in Abraham's life. You recall that at the critical moment, when Abraham took the knife in hand, ready to offer Isaac as a sacrifice, the Angel of God stayed his hand and told him that it was only a test of faith which he had met nobly and that Isaac's life was to be spared. Abraham then took a ram, which

1) Genesis, 22:1-13.

70

happened to pass at that moment, and in gratitude offered it as a substitute sacrifice.

In connection with this drama, there is an interesting Rabbinic legend which has impressed itself upon the conscience of our people.[2] Every part of this ram, which Abraham had offered as a sacrifice, was preserved by God for future use.[3] I shall limit myself to a reference to the use that was made of the ram's horns. "Of these two horns," we are told, "the Holy One, blessed be He, fashioned two *shofars*, or trumpets. With the left horn He sounded the message of *matan Torah*, the giving of the Torah — the Moral Law — on the mountain of Sinai, as it is written: 'And the sound of the *shofar* waxed louder and louder.'[4] And the right horn He will sound to herald *yeme hageulah*, the days of redemption, as it is written: 'And it shall come to pass on that day, a great trumpet shall be sounded.' "[5]

It is a fascinating comment which, I believe, has a pertinent message for us Jews and for the world at large in these trying times. There are *two shofars* which God wrought from the two horns of this historic ram. The trumpet sounds of both are equally important. We also hearken today to the shrill notes that come from the *shofar*, but these notes, if they are to be meaningful and effective, must symbolize for us both messages, the message of the giving of the Torah and the message of the Jew's and the world's redemption. One without the other does not fulfill the *shofar's* true purpose.

We Jews are today grateful that we have begun to hear the *shofar* of the *ge'ulah*, the trumpet proclaiming the redemption of our people. The ram's horn which God has kept all these

2) Pirke d'R. Eliezer, ch. 31.
3) For a fuller interpretation of the use made of each of these parts, see my sermon on "The Demands of the New Jewish World," in *A New World Is Born*, (N.Y., 1954), p. 173.
4) Exodus, 19:16, 19.
5) Isaiah, 27:13.

years has now been sounded. How long have we waited for that
call! I need not tell you that it is only what the Rabbis term the
aschalta d'ge'ulah, the beginning of the redemption. The State
of Israel is born, and we American Jews rejoice that we were
able to help in that rebirth. We acted the role of midwife; but
now something more is demanded of us. We must nurture the
child that it may grow, develop and prosper.

I do not wish to speak now of material needs but rather, to
emphasize a truth which the Rabbis urge us to grasp. We have
heard the sound of one *shofar*, that of redemption; now we
must listen to the sound of the second *shofar*, that of the giving of the Torah. To the Jew it is inconceivable that one can
do without the other. We do not want in Zion just another
state to dot the Near East; we want a State which will express
the Soul of the Jew! The body of the Jew has found its resting
place; now, in the words of the Psalmist, we must say :"Return,
O my soul unto they resting place!"[6]

There were two immortal founders of modern Zionism, The-
odor Herzl and Achad Ha-am; one complemented the other.
Herzl emphasized the State as the home of the scattered,
downtrodden people. Achad Ha-am visualized the Spiritual
Center, from which would radiate the sacred ideals of Israel
to Jews throughout the world. Herzl's dream has come true;
Achad Ha-am's vision must yet be realized. We want the words
of the prophet to be fulfilled: "For out of Zion shall go forth
the Law, and the word of the Lord from Jerusalem."[7] We thank
God that the leaders of modern Israel recognize this truth
and are striving to hearken to the *shofar* of *matan Torah*, not
only of the giving but also of the acceptance anew of the Divine Moral Law of life.

And this message of the two *shofars* comes to us American
Jews with special force. We, in America, as I have already said,

6) Psalms, 116:7
7) Isaiah, 2:3.

have helped in realizing the trumpet call of the *shofar* of redemption for our people in Israel. Now, we must concentrate on the call of the *shofar* for Torah here in America. Here in a sense we enjoy the blessings of redemption; we have the freedom and liberty which were denied us in most of the lands throughout the years of our exile. We have the opportunity now to enrich our spiritual life. Most of the five million Jews of America will remain in this land. We have to put meaning into our lives — Jewish meaning, Jewish content — in order to justify our lives here as Jews. We must produce a revival, a renascence of Jewish spiritual and cultural ideals, in order to be a blessing not only to ourselves but to America as well.

The Rabbis' legend of the two horns, has a message for our distraught and distressed world as well. The tragedy in which we find ourselves is due in large measure to this simple fact which our sages of old understood, and which *Rosh Hashanah* emphasizes, that there are two *shofars* which must be sounded and which must be heard if the world is to be saved. The call of redemption alone, without the call of Torah — the Moral Law — is a sham redemption, which must inevitably lead again to hatred, strife and war. If the world today is engulfed in darkness it is primarily because peoples and nations think they can achieve redemption without, at the same time, accepting the Moral Law.

We know, of course, that the Communist countries repudiate the Divine Moral Law. For them the State is the new god, to whom alone all obeisance is due, to whom the individual must surrender his mind, his lips, his heart, and his soul. But Communism has captivated the minds of many people in many lands, who live under economic, social, and political oppression, because they are led to believe that they are hearing the sounds of the trumpet of emancipation and redemption. They soon discover, however, that it is not the real *ge'ulah*.

Robert Louis Stevenson, in one of his writings, tells an allegory of a tribe of men who had been persuaded that it was foolish to wear shackles on their right ankles and so removed them; but the habit of being shackled was so strong, that before long they began to clamp the chains on their left ankles to replace those they had just removed from the right. So, here too, even those to whom the hope of economic redemption is offered exchange only one set of shackles for another which still holds them in bondage. It is not to Communism that the world can look for real redemption even if it could remove the shackles of physical bondage from the bodies of men. Without the Moral Law of genuine freedom and the recognition of the dignity of the human individual which the Law of Sinai proclaimed, it would be a change of but one bondage for another.

The democracies, on the other hand, do sound the trumpet of the Moral Law. Their governments rest on the principles which find their roots in the Law of Sinai. They have, however, failed to capture the minds of the masses in Asia, in Africa, even in South America. The reason is quite simple. They have thus far failed to sound with sufficient strength the *shofar* of *ge'ulah*, of redemption. They have not striven enough to help free the masses from the chains of bondage, political, social, economic, which have held them captive. Proclaiming the ideals of democracy to these people over the Voice of America, telling them we believe in the value of the moral principles of life, is good, but it is not enough. The needs of their stomachs are more immediate than the needs of their minds. When one is starved, naked, diseased or illiterate, the privileges of casting a vote has little appeal. America, fortunately, has begun to realize the importance of this truth. The Point Four Program in economic aid to countries endeavoring to ward off the menace of Communism was a step in the right direction. But here, too, in many cases, these efforts failed because this economic aid was used merely to increase military strength — and, in some instances only to maintain, those in power — instead of being used to advance the economic welfare of the masses, who remained in bondage. Aligning ourselves with rulers whose domestic policies serve only to keep the masses in shackles will again alienate those very masses whom we are striving so hard to influence, despite the millions we may pour into the coffers of their rulers.

But, above all, the democracies must show these enslaved masses that we ourselves believe in the Moral Law and live according to its Divine ideals. We must prove to them that we exemplify in our everyday lives those truths which we proclaim to them as inherent in democracy. The Communists make tremendous capital out of every failure of our professions of democracy. When we preach the equality and the dignity of man to the world's masses and then they hear about the horrible scenes enacted in some of our southern communities because of race prejudice, they instantly consider democracy a sham. And all our trumpet calls fail to touch their hearts. Alas, we fail to understand that every such dismal scene, which television vividly portrays and radio pointedly describes, helps to drive a nail in the coffin of democracy and world redemption.

Finally, there is a further insight which the Rabbinic tale of the two horns of the ram imparts to us. You recall that the sages tell us that "with the left horn God sounded the message of the giving of the Torah, and the right horn he will sound to herald the days of the redemption." The question naturally arises why the Rabbis assign a separate, specific purpose to the *left* horn and to the *right* horn. They could have said that one horn was for the proclamation of the Torah, and the other for redemption; evidently the words *left* and *right* may have a special significance for the modern world.[8]

The world today is divided into those on the left and those on the right. This is true not only in the economic sense but particularly in the field of politics and diplomacy. The lefts

8) I am indebted to an honored and revered friend and colleague, the late Rabbi Jacob Levinson, of blessed memory, for this interpretation, in his book, *Hadrash V'hahalakah*, (New York, 1950), p. 107.

may well refer to the Communists; the rights, to the democracies. Both are competing to win the hearts and minds of men. Both claim that they offer salvation to the world. Perhaps this old Rabbinic tale has a message for each. Not that the ancient sages foresaw such divisions in the world, but their emphasis on these two words gives us the right to interpret them in a modern sense. To those on the *left*, the Communists, the *left* horn of the ram, which was used at the giving of the Law of Sinai, proclaims the truth that all their claims for world redemption are in vain unless they also accept the Moral Law. To those on the *right*, the democracies, the *right* horn of the ram, which was to be sounded at the advent of the Messiah, proclaims the truth that all their claims for the moral values of life will be ineffective unless they are faithful, in fullest measure, to the *shofar's* call for redemption.

Whichever group sounds and obeys the calls of both *shofars* — the trumpet of Torah and the trumpet of *ge'ulah* — will hold the key to world salvation.

As Jews and as Americans we have the implicit faith that the democracies will hearken to this vital message of the ancient seers which holds out the one hope for the world today.

Amalek and Haman — A Study in Contrast

A Purim sermon, preached Sabbath morning, March 1, 1947. It recalls a phase in British-Jewish Palestine relationship during the administration of the Labor Government, now, happily a matter of past history. The sermon is inserted as a reminder of historic incidents which should not be altogether forgotten.

The Sabbath preceding the festival of Purim bears a special designation in the Jewish calendar. It is referred to as *Shabbat Zakor* — the Sabbath of Remembering — and it derives its name from the fact that on this Sabbath we read an additional portion of the Torah which begins with the word *Zakor*, "Remember what Amalek did unto thee on the way, as ye came forth out of Egypt!"[1]

It has always seemed strange to me that the Rabbis selected this particular portion to be read on the Sabbath before Purim. Haman, the villain of the Purim story, was indeed assumed to be a descendant of the Amalekites. But after all, Amalek was not one of the greatest enemies of our people. The attack which the Amalekites had waged against us was not one of the severest which our ancestors experienced, indeed, the enemy was quickly overpowered. It would have been much more logical, it would appear, for the Rabbis to have selected a chapter reminding us of what the Pharaohs had done to us in keeping us enslaved for centuries. Why remember just Amalek?

It seems to me that our sages had a definite purpose in mind.

---

1) Deuteronomy, 25:17.

They desired that just before we consider Haman, we remind ourselves of another type of enemy whose eventual aim was the same, but whose approach, whose method, whose technique was altogether different.

Haman was a villain. He hated the Jews and was determined to bring about their destruction. He did not conceal his enmity but was outspoken in his aims. He proclaimed to all the king's provinces that they were "to destroy, to slay, and to cause to perish all Jews, both young and old, little children and women."[2]

Hitler was such a Haman. He made no effort to conceal his deep hatred of the Jew. He boasted about his methods of solving the Jewish question, cruel as they were, and was loud in his open declarations that he came to eradicate the Jew from the face of the earth. Thank God, he too met Haman's fate. He and his vicious cohorts are gone, let us hope, forever!

Amalek, however, was a different kind of enemy. The Rabbis in the Midrash give us an altogether different picture of the Amalek one sees in a superficial reading of the Bible story. According to these sages, Amalek did not profess to be an enemy at all. In fact he claimed kinship to Israel,[3] and because of such relationship he pretended to be a friend of the Israelites. Before attacking them, he lured them with kindly words.[4] He did not attack them openly; nay, he lay in ambush, and in this hidden fashion he kept molesting the Jews. The Rabbis see the Amalekite technique in the very name of his cohorts, *Am lak*, "They came to suck the blood of Israel."[5] At length, Amalek gave up this game of hide and seek and with a bold front openly revealed himself an enemy of Israel!

Nay, more, Amalek, according to our Rabbis, was an ex-

2) Esther, 3:13.
3) Tanchuma, Ki Teze, 9; Pesikta d'Rav Kahana (ed.Buber 1868), p. 27a.
4) *Ibid.*
5) *Ibid.*

pert magician and hoped through tricks of magic to bring about Israel's destruction.[6]

Unlike Haman, who attacked the Jews living in their own homes, comfortably settled in the land of their adoption, Amalek attacked the Jews *baderek*, "on the way", as they wandered, homeless, just liberated from the yoke of Pharaoh. He did not attack the strong among them; on the contrary, "he smote the hindmost of them, all that were enfeebled, faint and weary."[7] The Amalekites were not an ordinary people. They were not a backward, unknown tribe; *reshit goyim Amalek*, says the Bible, "Amalek was first among the nations,"[8] a leader among the peoples of the world. And herein lay the greatest disappointment; that this *reshit goyim*, this leader among nations, this supposed friend of Israel, should turn upon her in such a treacherous manner.

How history does at times repeat itself! *Zakor Amalek!* Remember Amalek! Now, when the Jew has finally seen the end of the modern Pharaoh; now, when he has begun to breathe the air of freedom, having broken the shackles of modern Egypt; now, alas, Amalek appears to destroy the very hope that gave the Jew the strength and the courage to withstand the agonies of all these years of the cruel Hitler.

And whom does this modern Amalek attack? Those who are *baderek* — "on the way," homeless, displaced persons, wandering without a roof over their heads! *Kol hanecheshalim*, "Those who have fallen by the wayside," those who are enfeebled and weakened from all their travail during these many years. And when is this attack aimed? *V'atah ayef v'yagea*, "When thou art tired and weary," so weary and so tired after the loss of six millions of our brethren and after we have been drained of our last bit of strength! And who plays the role of

6) Talmud Jerusalem, Rosh Hashanah, 3,59a. Cf. L. Ginzberg, *Legends*, vol. 6. p. 24, note 144.
7) Deuteronomy, 25:18.
8) Numbers, 24:20.

Amalek today? *reshit goyim*, "the leader among nations,"
Great Britain, standard bearer of freedom and liberty! It pains
me to say that this *reshit goyim*, foremost of civilized peoples, has today become the *am lak*, the people draining the
last bit of blood from the already blood-drenched children of
Israel!

And the strangest part of it all is that, like their ancient
prototype, this modern Amalek claimed to be a kinsman to
the leaders of Jewish Palestine. Until the leaders of the Labor
Party came into power they prided themselves on their relationship with the labor leaders of the *Yishuv*. They pretended
to be friends of Jewish Palestine, and they lulled us with sweet
words into believing that they were comrades with us in our
ideal. And now, after coming into power, they suddenly reveal
themselves as the modern Amalek!

And their method is also that of the *am lak*, the people
that sucketh our blood! Lying in ambush, stirring up acts of
terroism and then blaming the Jew for that very terrorism
which by their criminal acts they produce themselves. And
like the old Amalek, they have become master magicians,
and with tricks of magic have brought havoc upon the Jews
in Palestine as well as upon all our brethren now languishing
in the displaced persons' camps. Creating the Anglo-Ameri-
can Commission was their trick of magic. They never intended to abide by its decision; it was mere trickery to deceive an
unsuspecting world! They themselves organized the Arab
League to serve their devilish purposes, and now again with
the magician's wand they pose this League as the arbiter of
Palestine's fate. The recent outburst of Ernest Bevin, stripped
of all its vulgarity and impudence, was another trick of magic
with which he had hoped to shift the blame of failure from
himself to the shoulders of President Truman. And now, the
master magic trick, the turning over of the Palestine case to
the United Nations, again, nothing more or less than a sleight
of hand to fool the world. Already, Bevin has announced that

Britain will not be bound by the decision of the United Nations, that they are referring the matter merely for advice and nothing more.

Oh, the hypocrisy of Amalek! In this respect Bevin is just like Haman himself. You recall that when Haman, after having been invited to attend Queen Esther's banquet, joyfully recounted to his wife and friends the glory and the honor that came to him, he said: "Yet all this availeth me nothing, so long as I see Mordecai the Jew sitting at the king's gate."[9] The Rabbis in the Talmud see an altogether different meaning in these words. They translate the phrase *yoshev b'shaar hamelek*, that "Mordecai was sitting at the gate of the king's Court of Justice," pleading the cause of his unfortunate people. But Haman, seeing him attempting to plead for justice, mockingly said: "All this bothers me little," for *zeh ba b'pruzbuli, vze ba b'pruzbuti*, "he comes as a pleader with legal claims of justice, but I come with envoys, with diplomats!"[10]

How true a description of Bevin's motives in handing over the Palestine case to the United Nations! The Jew sitting at this Gate of World Justice, hoping for justice to his people, troubles Bevin very little. He, too, like Haman, undoubtedly says, *kol zeh enenu shaveh li*, "All this does not bother me! For the Jew comes only *b'pruzbuli*, with the claims of legality and morality, whereas I appear *b'pruzbuti*, with my diplomats, the Arab delegates whom I have created, and my other satellites whom I support!"

What a tragic role for Great Britain to play today! Oh, how the mighty have fallen! What a transformation from the Britain of Balfour and Lloyd George to the Britain of Attlee and Bevin, from the Britain *shel maalah*, the exalted, lofty Britain that won the world's esteem, to the Britain *shel matah*,

9) Esther, 5:13.
10) Megillah, 15a.

the lowly, unworthy Britain, the product of its Foreign and Colonial Ministries!

What can the Jew do now? The Biblical account of Israel's battle with Amalek gives us the answer. Moses said to Joshua: "Choose us men, and go out to fight with Amalek!"[11] The Rabbis interpret this command of Moses in greater detail. What kind of men were to be chosen for this battle? R. Joshua said: *anashim gibborim*, "mighty men," men of valor and of heroic stature. R. Eliezer said: *anashim yir'e chet*, "men who fear to commit sin,"[12] men who abhor acts that are sinful. Both of these qualifications are essential if victory is to be ours.

Thank God, Palestine Jewry represents *anashim gibborim*. We may indeed be proud of the mighty deeds of heroism which are being enacted by the Jews of Palestine. We behold in these Jews the true descendants of the ancient Maccabees. The entire *Yishuv*, represented by the *Haganah*, is ready to offer its life to preserve what the Jews have fashioned by their sweat and blood in their old-new land. We have *gibborim*, ready to defend their people and their land against every attack of Amalek.

And we are thankful, too, that the vast majority of the *Yishuv* recognize also the truth of R. Eliezer's dictum that our mighty men must also be *yir'e chet*. The moral law is in force for them even in time of battle. Killing British soldiers, bombing buildings, is not part of their program of battle. The Irgun and the Stern groups have not succeeded in capturing the approval of the mass of our struggling people, even though the brutality of the modern Amalek is enough to drive men to madness. We cannot altogether blame these *gibborim*, driven to acts of violence by the persistent injustice of an Amalekite policy. We can understand them, but shall not follow them. We shall still cling to the motto: *anashim yir'e chet*.

11) Exodus, 17:9.
12) Mekilta, (ed. Lauterbach) 2:141.

We shall refuse to be perpetrators of acts that are sinful. We still believe that Zion will be, must be, redeemed in justice! To help Jews enter Palestine, to get ships to unload their living cargo on that sacred soil, the Jews in Eretz Yisrael will fight and will be ready to give their lives. But the *gevurah*, the might of our brethren in Eretz Yisrael, shall always be inspired by the sacred impulse of *yirat chet*, the refusal to be sharers in sin.

And the Bible story has also a message for us American Jews. You recall that while Joshua and his men were battling Amalek, Moses, though not in actual battle, stood atop a mountain, observing from the distance the heroic struggle of his people. "And it came to pass, when Moses held up his hand, that Israel prevailed; and when he let down his hand Amalek prevailed."[13] Yea, here is the task for American Jewry, who, like Moses, must watch this great struggle from the distance. We must stand on the mountaintop. We must lift ourselves out of our petty, everyday concerns and rise to the heights of Zionist idealism and vision. But above all, and again like Moses, we must lift up our hands in constant effort and labor, cooperating with our brethren from afar, giving all possible encouragement and support. As long as our hands are lifted high in the service of our ideal, *v'gavar Yisrael*, Israel will be victorious.

The Bible adds a dramatic note to the picture which we have described. "Moses' hands were heavy; and they took a stone and put it under him, and he sat thereon."[14] And the Rabbis pointedly ask: "Why did they put a stone for Moses to sit thereon? Could they not find something soft upon which he might rest?" And they answer that Moses said: "As long as my people finds itself *b'tzaar*, in sorrow, in misery, *af ani eheye imahem b'tzaar*, I, too, want to feel with them their anguish and their pain!"[15] That must be the attitude of American Jewry to-

13) Exodus, 17:11.
14) *Ibid.*, v. 12.
15) Rashi, *ibid.*; Taanit, 11a.

day. As long as our people are called upon to endure suffering and pain in their struggle for the rebirth of their national life and national home, we, too, must willingly, sacrificially, feel with them and share with them their *tzaar* and agony.

Thus we may hope that the Biblical promise will again be fulfilled. The memory of the cruelties of this Amalek, too, will be utterly blotted out from under heaven, and to the Jews in Eretz Yisrael and throughout the world there shall again be "light and gladness, joy and honor!"[16]

16) *Cf.* Esther, 8:16.

The Ten Plagues
and Their Modern Significance

Preached on the first day of Passover,
April 16, 1957.

One of the important aspects of the story of the Exodus from Egyptian bondage is the tale of the ten plagues which God inflicted upon Pharaoh and the Egyptians in order to force the liberation of the enslaved Israelites.

There is something strange in this account, which is usually passed over unnoticed, but which, if studied, can provide us with a new insight into the entire episode. After each of the first few plagues which Moses and Aaron, at the behest of God, had brought about, Pharaoh summoned his *chartumim*, his magicians, and, lo and behold, "the magicians of Egypt with their secret arts, did exactly the same."[1] We should imagine that the Bible would hide, rather than reveal, this fact which seems to belittle the miracle which Moses and Aaron displayed. But the Bible emphasizes a deeper truth. Anyone can bring plagues into the world. God visited these plagues upon Egypt because evil had to be punished, but men, too, can bring plagues upon themselves. The only magic required for these is the magic of cruelty and tyranny.

The difficulty is not how to infest the world with plagues but how to cure the world of them. For the question immediately arises, why did not Pharaoh summon these same magicians to stop the plagues which Moses had brought upon his land? If their magic was so great as to be able to duplicate the

1) Exodus, 7:11, 22; 8:3.

plagues, why could they not put an end to them once they appeared? But this is the point of the whole story. It is easy to bring plagues into the world. The real art is *how to put an end* to plagues. And this art the Egyptian magicians did not possess.

For thousands of years cruel men, tyrants, have brought countless plagues upon the world. In our own lifetime we have seen Hitler turn rivers into blood, Stalin turn light into darkness for millions of human beings; just recently we saw Soviet magicians perform their cruel arts in Hungary; and now Nasser, the present Egyptian Pharaoh, threatens our world with similar plagues. All these despots, "with their secret arts," possessed, or still possess, this gift of hurling plagues upon the world. Alas, we have not yet learned the art of putting an end to these plagues. Why? Why, at at this state of our civilization, have we failed to bring about an end to these plagues which afflict our world?

Notice in the Biblical tale that Pharaoh himself called on Moses to end the plagues, for Moses alone possessed this power. Not that he was a more expert magician; not that he was more skillful in "the secret arts." The answer is quite simple. He was not a "magician" at all. He was the mouthpiece of God, standing at the side of God; and God was standing at his side.

The Hebrew text of the Bible tale is most revealing on this theme. When God sent Moses on his historic mission, He said to him: *Bo el Pharaoh,* "Go unto Pharaoh."[2] Again and again in this story we read these same words. But anyone with even a beginner's knowledge of Hebrew knows that the word *bo* does not mean *go,* it means *come.* The Hebrew word for *go* is *lek,* and the text should have read *lek el Pharaoh,* not *bo el Pharaoh!*

Here is an interesting lesson in elementary Hebrew. If I wish

2) *Ibid.,* 7:26; 9:1; 10:1.

to send someone on an errand, I would say *lek*, *go*. But if I want someone to accompany me on the errand, I would say *bo*, *come*, just as this thought would be implicit in English, were I to say, "Come!"

In other words, what the Hebrew text in the Bible tells us is that Moses accompanied God on his misssion to Pharaoh, and that God accompanied him. Moses did not go alone or speak his own words; he spoke God's words, he was but the bearer of God's truth. The Rabbis put it still more clearly when they tell us that "the Holy One, blessed be He, *haya medaber mitok grono shel Moshe*, spoke through the throat of Moses."[3]

Thus we better understand one aspect of our own tragedy. We fail to cure the world of its plagues because, in all the dealings of the nations, it is the "secret arts" that we employ, it is the matching of magical wits, it is not the voice of God that is being heard!

That this should be the policy of the Communist regimes is no surprise. They have openly repudiated God and God's truth. Brute force is their bible! But, alas, with pain in our hearts, we must admit that this is also true in the case of the democratic powers. In all their dealings with the dictators of our age, they did not hear God's voice saying, *bo el Pharaoh* "Come with Me to the Pharaoh," but heeded the call, *lek*, *go* on your own!

The truth can now be told. All students of the Hitlerian era make it very clear that the democracies too had their share in the making of Hitler. In all their dealings with him, from his first appearance as a prospective enemy of the world until the

---

3) An oft-quoted teaching in the work of medieval Rabbis, though the source is unknown. Very likely it is a paraphrase of the statement found in Mekilta, Bachodesh, 4, (ed. Jacob Z. Lauterbach, II, p. 223). Cf. also Zohar, to Exodus, 19:19. The Mohammedans also employ this expression with reference to Moses. Cf. I. Goldziher, *La Notion de la Sekina*, p. 12, note 2.

historic meeting in Munich, it was always *lek el Hitler*, not God's voice urging *bo el Hitler!* Each nation looked out only for its own interest, how to utilize the villain against others, thinking thereby to save only itself.

With all our affection for the late President Roosevelt and our admiration for Winston Churchill, we must, alas, acknowledge, as the records now show, that when they sat face to face with Stalin at Yalta, it was not God's voice that always spoke through their lips; again, it was *lek el Stalin* not *bo el Stalin*, coming as the messengers of God. It was a play upon a diplomatic chessboard, again, the "secret arts" of one versus the "secret arts" of the other. Is there any wonder that the plague of bloodletting could not be stopped?

And now in the nations' dealings with the modern Pharaoh, Nasser, again it is not *bo el Nasser*, going to him with God at one's side, speaking God's words, but *lek el Nasser*, uttering one's own magical words, matching wits, forgetting the Rabbinic saying that when it comes to magic, "there are no magicians anywhere to match the magicians of Egypt."[4] The very word diplomacy has lost its ideal meaning and purpose, dealings between nations based upon justice and truth, and has come to be recognized as dealings between nations based upon shrewdness, trickery and *lehatim*, "the secret arts."

Could anyone have imagined that the United States, the world's greatest proponent of democracy, would enter into a treaty with another nation in which she would be a party to open discrimination against a large number of her own citizens? When Czarist Russia, half a century ago, refused to recognize an American passport held by a Jew and thus denied him entry into Russia, America rose to the occasion and broke off all its commercial treaties with that country at great financial loss to the American economy. It did so because it firmly believed that no financial gain is worth the price of such

4) Abot d'R. Nathan, (ed. Schechter) Version I, ch. 28. p. 43a.

discrimination toward any of its citizens. That was God's voice speaking through American authorities. Yet today we enter into a treaty with Saudi Arabia, putting the seal of the United States to a clause which prohibits American soldiers of the Jewish faith from being stationed at a United States Air Force Base in that land. Again it was not *bo el King Saud*, but *lek*, not accompanied by God and Godliness but going alone, with the discredited secret arts of the old time Egyptian magic.

And, alas, the same holds true even in the United Nations. We Jews have always believed in and hoped for a United Nations. In the liturgy for our High Holy Days we have a beautiful prayer which we have repeated for centuries, praying for the coming of the day when "all the nations will form an *agudah achat*, one union." But our prayer did not conclude with these words alone. It added the significant phrase, "to do Thy will with a sincere heart!" Alas, this part of the prayer has not yet been fulfilled. We have a United Nations, but the participants in the main are far from performing in accord with the ideal, "to do Thy will with a sincere heart." Self interest, not righteousness or truth, is the test by which measures are judged. Nations decide issues not upon their just merits, but by the interest of blocs — we have the Communist bloc, the Western bloc, the Arab bloc, the Afro-Asian bloc — each guided by its own selfish interest, not by God's measure of truth.

Here, then is one of the tragedies of our age; and here is the message of the old Passover story. And until the world learns that message we shall continue to be plagued by the horrors that we behold today.

Armaments alone will not cure the plagues. Neither jet planes nor nuclear warheads will achieve that result; on the contrary, the plagues will only multiply. Only when nations and the United Nations learn to speak God's words, to stand at the side of God, will all the modern Pharaohs be vanquished. Then will the world's plagues disappear and the sunshine of true redemption come to all the peoples of the earth.

The Prophet Ezekiel's Message to a Modern World Struggling For Freedom

Preached on the first day of Passover,
March 27, 1956.

It is interesting to observe that the Jew begins to think of the dramatic struggle for human freedom, which the festival of Passover commemorates, long before the fifteenth day of *Nissan*, the official date of the holiday. The Sabbath preceding that historic date bears a special designation in the Jewish calendar, *Shabbat Hagadol*, "the Great Sabbath." On that day our thoughts are directed to the Passover of the future, when Elijah the prophet will herald the dawn of the Messianic era of universal freedom and peace. In some communities on that Great Sabbath, the Jews read parts of the *Haggadah* usually reserved for the Seder eve, in order to attune their minds to the ideal of freedom, and so better to appreciate how freedom is to be achieved and what freedom demands of us.

Indeed, the Jew is enjoined to concentrate his thoughts on freedom even before the Great Sabbath. More than two weeks before the festival, on the Sabbath on which we usher in the month of *Nissan*, we are also bidden to focus our thoughts on the struggle for human freedom. That Sabbath, too, bears a special designation, *Shabbat Hachodesh*, and once more, through Torah and Scriptural readings, we are asked to give thought to the concept of human freedom, to note what is required of us, as individuals and as a nation, if the dream of man's freedom is to become a reality. The Jew has always instinctively understood that human freedom cannot be achieved spontaneously. We must consider its many aspects,

90

we must plan for it, we must purify ourselves from all the de-
filements which obstruct the achievement of freedom.

Let us, therefore, turn our minds this morning to the *Haftorah* or Scriptural lesson which we read on the *Shabbat Hachodesh*, the Sabbath which precedes the festive month of
Nissan, and which is taken from the prophecies of Ezekiel.
This prophet was among the captives driven into Babylon after
the first destruction of the Temple and Jerusalem. Ezekiel en-
deavoured to instill within the hearts of the captives the hope
for a future redemption. He describes for them in detail the
new Jerusalem and the Temple which will be rebuilt. He even
goes into an elaborate description of the ritual to be enacted in the Temple, especially on the days preceding the festival of Passover. Part of this ritual is new and not set forth in
the Pentateuch. Evidently captivity had taught the prophet
wherein Israel had failed and what had to be done, once the
restoration came, if freedom was to be assured.

"On the first day of the first month," Ezekiel declares, a
sacrifice should be offered, "and thou shalt purify the sanctuary."[1] This is something new, something novel, that the
Sanctuary itself must be purified. Nay, again, on the seventh
day of the month, this is to be repeated, not only for sins wittingly committed but also for the sins *me'ish shogeh u'mipesi*,
"of one that erreth and of him that is simple; so shall ye make
atonement for the House."[2] Here is a teaching that you will
not find in any other religion or in the annals of any other people, that the House of God needs periodic purification to see
that it is an instrument working for the freedom of man. It too
requires atonement for sins of commission or omission which
may have hindered the triumph of freedom. What a remarkable concept this is! Before a people celebrates a festival dedicated to freedom, religion itself must go through a process of

1) Ezekiel, 45:18.
2) *Ibid.*, v. 20.

purification, and its Houses of God must make atonement for failures to help achieve freedom for mankind.

Truly, the world needs this teaching today! In our own Southern states a battle is raging to free the Negro from the vestiges of degradation that afflict him. How silent the Church has been in this effort to win true freedom for people whose only sin is that their skin is black! What a travesty on religion that a Negro cannot enter even a House of God in which white people are seated! President Eisenhower, at his recent press conference gave a fitting rebuke to these "Houses of God" when he said that he looked to the pulpits of the Churches to take the lead in teaching the people the need for accepting the decision of the Supreme Court in the matter of desegregation. It is to the credit of the Catholic Church that it is at least making a beginning "to purify the House" and to make atonement for these sins of the past.

In celebrating the festival of our freedom from bondage, we Jews have been taught to think of all the enslaved, Jews and nonJews alike. When Moses appeared before Pharaoh to plead for the redemption of his brethren, he at the same time pleaded the cause of freedom for all slaves. No wonder that the Bible tells us, "The man Moses became very great also in the land of Egypt, in the sight of the slaves of Pharaoh, and in the sight of all the people."[3] Yea, not only the Israelites went free, but "a mixed multitude went up also with them!"[4] We Jews feel the pangs of humiliation when any segment of the population is still in bondage, and we know that a religion is not true to itself if it fails to lead in the struggle for human liberation.

But I wish to come closer to home and to look at the struggle in which our people are now engaged, to win their full freedom in the reborn land of Israel. How few, alas, are the Houses of God of our Christian neighbors which give expression of en-

3) Exodus, 11:3.
4) *Ibid.*, 12:38.

couragement to our embattled brethren in the great crisis which they face.

Some of you may have read a letter, recently published, written by the Rev. Edward L. Elson, the minister of the National Presbyterian Church in Washington, in which President Eisenhower is a worshiper. Reports, widely circulated, allege that Rev. Elson is a member of the notorious American Friends of the Near East, which in reality should be termed the American Haters of Israel, and that he has had some influence over President Eisenhower concerning his decisions in the present struggle in the Middle East. A woman from Chicago, a Mrs. Lowenthal, wrote to the minister and bluntly asked him whether there was any truth to these reports. Rev. Elson answered that he is the spiritual advisor to the President, not his political advisor (though he did not state whether he regarded the present struggle in the Middle East as a spiritual or a political matter). And then he continued in familiar fashion, to state that he is no enemy of the Jews, some of his best friends are Jews, as an army chaplain he had officiated for the Jewish men in the absence of a Jewish chaplain, but that he "is desperately and earnestly pro-American, and that political Zionism does violence to that concept." "The German-American Bund was out of place in American life," he wrote, "and so are Zionist American organizations."

Here is a representative of religion, the minister of one of the most important churches in the land, who has the distinction of serving the spiritual needs of the President of the United States, who cannot see a difference between the traitorous German-American Bund working for the victory of the enemy of all democratic governments, including our own, doing their utmost to establish Nazism here in America, and the Zionists whose ideal is to help re-establish a wandering, tortured people in their historic homeland, there to build a citadel of genuine democracy.

Oh, for an Ezekiel in our day to proclaim the need: "And

thou shalt purify the Sanctuary!" What a shallow, perverted conception of patriotism this representative of the House of God reveals! Just a week ago on St. Patrick's Day, we saw, as we looked on the television screen, a quarter of a million Irish-Americans marching on Fifth Avenue and also saw at least three-quarters of a million standing on the sidewalks watching the procession; we heard the news commentator, describing the scene, tell us of the pride on the faces of these Irish-Americans as they recalled the heroism and martyrdom of the patriots in Ireland fighting for their freedom. Would the reverend gentleman of Washington dare to impugn the patriotism of these fellow-American citizens of Irish ancestry?

Just last Saturday, one-hundred-thousand Americans of Greek descent marched on the same avenue to celebrate the anniversary of Greek independence, and an equal number of Greek-Americans on the sidewalks greeted the paraders. Floats were displayed reviewing the struggle of Greek liberation from the Turks, and also the struggle of the Greeks in Cyprus for union with Greece. Some of the floats were not at all complimentary to our British ally whom they are battling in Cyprus. Would the Rev. Elson dare to compare the loyalty of the Greek-Americans with the disloyalty of the German-American Bund? Alas, only in the case of the Jew, working for that noble Zionist ideal which won the recognition of statesmen like Lloyd George, Balfour and Churchill in England, and of every President of the United Statees beginning with Woodrow Wilson, does a minister of God dare to challenge his loyalty and patriotism! If we be gracious and say that such criticism is not a deliberate defilement of God's Sanctuary, certainly we can describe it in Ezekiel's words, as a sin, *me'ish shogeh u'mipesi*, "of one who erreth and of one that is simple."

Does this minister, the voice of his House of God, help the cause of human freedom in thwarting the existence of Israel? When the State Department of our government approved the shipment of tanks to Saudi Arabia, did this minister utter a word of protest, knowing the use to which these tanks would be put? Is Saudi Arabia a country where democratic ideals are fostered? Just the other day, a dispatch from London appeared in *The New York Times*, in which King Saud is named as Saudi Arabia's foremost patron of the extensive slave-hunting flourishing on the Persian Gulf coasts. The Anti-Slavery and Aborigines Protection Society, which issued the report, endorsed its authenticity and accuracy. And this is the man to whom America sends tanks and arms to defend democracy! And it is such action that this representative of the Sanctuary would want American Jews to approve in order to attest to their loyalty.

Somehow, men of this type cannot understand that the interests of Israel are identical with the interests of America, that Israel is the one bastion of genuine democracy in that area of feudalism, autocracy, and dictatorship, and that the Zionists in America are working for the loftiest ideals of democracy when they work for the preservation and development of the State of Israel. We have heard the Houses of God resound with protests when the Communists endeavored to penetrate the borders of other lands. And yet, see how silent their voices have become when Communist arms and personnel penetrated Egypt to help destroy the one fortress of human freedom in that region. Yea, how vital is Ezekiel's message today, "Ye shall make atonement for the House," for the failure of the Houses of God to defend God's truth, the truth of human freedom!

Our prophet, however, goes further in prescribing the rituals to be enacted in the New Jerusalem on the days preceding Passover, the Festival of Freedom. Not only was the Sanctuary to be purified and to seek atonement, but "on that day, the *Nasi*, the prince, shall prepare for himself and for all the people of the land a sin offering."[5] Here, again, is something unique,

5) *Ibid.*, v. 22.

unparalleled in the history of other religions or peoples. Before you can celebrate a meaningful festival of freedom, the *Nasi*, the layleader of the community, must also purify himself, must search and examine his soul to see whether his actions and the actions of those under him have helped or hindered the cause of freedom. No man is perfect, and the layleader, with all the good intentions that he may have, must nevertheless make atonement not only for the failings and sins that are committed wittingly, but also for those committed by "one who erreth and one that is simple."

With all due respect to the *Nasi* of America, President Eisenhower, we may truthfully say that he too might heed the Prophet's injunction. Certainly, we do not charge that he wilfully hindered the cause of freedom, but we do say and have a right to say that the actions of some of his important aides are those which Ezekiel describes as the actions "of one who erreth and of him that is simple."

When Secretary Dulles tells the Senate that he does not favor the request of Israel for arms because he wants to prevent an arms race, we indeed can say that these are words of one who erreth. There is an arms race now, not a race between Israel and the Arab nations, but a race between the Western Powers and the Communist countries as to who should have the privilege of supplying the Arab nations with arms. Israel does not seek a race in arms nor does she ask for arms to match the Communist shipments to Egypt. She asks for defensive weapons only to halt and to prevent the work of destruction should the Communist weapons be used. Or is the Secretary such a *pesi*, so simple, that he thinks Nasser will use these Communist arms to fight the Communists?

And when Secretary Dulles tells the Senate that Israel, with a million-and-a-half inhabitants, cannot expect to match the arms necessary for forty million Arabs, we again wonder whether the Prophet's description is not true, that these are words of "one who erreth and of one that is simple." Certainly, Dulles would not use that criterion in judging the propriety of America's supplying arms to the little island of Formosa to protect it against the hundreds of millions in Red China.

But perhaps we are too charitable to our Secretary of State when we describe his actions in those mild words of the Prophet Ezekiel. When in that same session with the Senate Committee the Secretary tried to explain the Arab's hatred of the Jew by the unfounded charge that the Jews had killed Mohammed, a charge which caused laughter even among the Arabs, we think a harsher term than Ezekiel's could be used. And when, on his visit to Nasser in Cairo some three years ago, he presented the Egyptian premier with a pearl-studded pistol as a symbol of American friendship, we say again that Ezekiel's words are far too mild to describe such action, one that certainly does not betoken America's yearning for human freedom. When Dr. Weizmann, of blessed memory, visited President Truman in the White House, he presented to him a *Sefer Torah*, a scroll of God's Law, as a token of Israel's friendship to America. What a contrast in understanding national aspirations for freedom and peace between the gift of a *Sefer Torah* and that of a pistol, even if it be studded with pearls. Yea, there is great need for the Prophet's injunction: "the *Nasi*, the prince, shall prepare for himself," and we add, especially for those under him, "a sin offering."

When we criticize the policy of our beloved country, we do so with pain in our hearts. When we find fault with her present outlook on the Middle East, it is because we are interested not in Israel alone but in the weal of America as well, because we are convinced that the interests of the two countries coincide. When we raise our voices in behalf of Israel it is not because of lack of loyalty or patriotism to America; on the contrary it is because we so love America that we want to see her uphold the loftiest ideals of justice and righteousness in the struggle to achieve human freedom. When a parent upbraids his child it is not because he dislikes the child, but because he loves him

and wants him to correct his ways. The wise author of the Book
of Proverbs has told us that "the father correcteth the son in
whom he delighteth."[6]

A great sage of the Talmud, Rabbi Shila, once uttered this
beautiful blessing: "Blessed art Thou, O Lord, who hast given
us a government on earth that resembles the government in
the heavens!"[7] We Jews, and we Zionists, want to offer this
benediction for America: "Blessed art Thou, O Lord, who
hast granted us this government on earth, America, which reflects the beauty of God's government in the heavens!"

And so, too, with reference to the *Nasi* of our country. It
is because we revere our President so highly, because we
have such deep affection and regard for him, that we would
want him to typify the noblest and purest in the American
ideal of freedom. Our Bible pays a beautiful tribute to King
Solomon, saying of him: "And Solomon sat on the throne of
God."[8] The Rabbis were surprised when they read this verse,
and they asked, "Can it ever be said that a human being sits
on the throne of God?" But they answered wisely: "Yes, God's
throne is the throne of justice and righteousness. And any
one who is guided by these Divine ideals, sits on God's
throne."[9] We wish to be able to say, and we wish history to record, that our beloved President "sits on the throne of God!"

America is playing a leading role in the world's struggle for
freedom. Peoples still enslaved look to America for bold and
lofty leadership. The struggle for the preservation of that bastion of democracy, the State of Israel, and America's role in
this struggle, will test whether America can win the hearts of
all those who now put their trust in her.

May the representatives of the Houses of God and the lay

6) Proverbs, 3:12.
7) Berakot, 58a.
8) I Chronicles, 29:23.
9) Yalkut Shimoni, *ibid.*, Metzudat Davi, *ibid.*; Pesikta Rabbati,
    (ed. M. Friedman), p. 77a.

leaders of the democratic governments heed the words of the Prophet Ezekiel; may there be a purification of heart and mind and a sincere atonement for errors committed. Then we shall be able to hope for the dawn of a new Passover, when the prayer, in the words of the *Haggadah*, of all who are still shackled and enslaved will be answered: "This year we are slaves, may the coming year find us free men!"

———————

Judaism
and the Problem of Evil

Address delivered at B'nai B'rith Summer Institute, Starlight, Pa., July 3, 1959, and printed in the Autumn, 1959 issue of *Jewish Heritage*, published by the B'nai B'rith Department of Adult Jewish Education.

Judaism is a unique religion because it is a way of life. Its stress is on the world of here and now, on morality and conduct rather than on dogma or creed. Unlike many other religions, it imposes no fixed set of beliefs or authoritarian theology through which man must try to win salvation. It is not surprising, therefore, that Judaism offers no single explanation for one of humanity's greatest and most perplexing enigmas: what is the meaning and purpose of evil and human suffering.

Indeed, the concept of evil is one of the most difficult subjects dealt with in Jewish thought. As Dr. Kaufmann Kohler, the eminent Jewish scholar and theologian has put it: "A leading objection to the belief in Divine Providence is the existence in this world of physical and moral evil."[1] Professor Isaac Husik, in his classic work, A *History of Medieval Jewish Philosophy*, places the problem in historic perspective: "The presence of evil in this world, physical and moral, was a stumbling block to all religious thinkers in the Middle Ages."[2] Today, also, the existence of evil makes it hard for many to believe in a divine power.

There are various aspects to the subject. First there is the problem of evil in the mind and nature of man. Why was man

1) Dr. K. Kohler, *Jewish Theology*, (N.Y., 1918), p. 176.
2) P. 288.

created with the desire to do evil? Why should God, the God of goodness, have created within man the temptation to do evil?

To the Rabbis this question did not pose a problem at all because in their understanding of human nature they did not conceive of man as inherently angelic. While man was given an evil inclination, the *yetzer hara*; he was also given a counter-force, the *yetzer tov*, a good impulse. And God challenges man to choose which will prevail, the evil or the good.

One of the basic teachings of Judaism is that man has a free will, the power to choose between evil and good. In the Bible God says to man, "Behold, I have set before thee life and good, death and evil. . . . Choose life."[3] We are placed on earth to wage this battle within ourselves and to try to conquer our evil inclination. The Rabbis even advise us that if the impulse to do evil should become strong and overpowering, compelling us to commit a sin or a crime, we are to seize the *yetzer hara* and take it to the synagogue, the House of Study, where, by immersion in prayer and study, we can conquer it.[4]

This conflict is illustrated in the Biblical passage where Jacob, sleeping on a bed of rocks, dreams of the ladder that touches the earth and reaches to the heavens. The Bible says that he saw angels "ascending and descending *bo*, on it"; but, as the Rabbis suggest, the Hebrew word *bo* does not mean "*on it*", but "*in him*," in Jacob.[5] In other words, the Rabbis interpret the story to emphasize the thought that there were two forces struggling *bo*, within Jacob, one leading him heavenward, the other pulling him downward. Jacob, like all of us, contained this struggle within himself. The answer of the Rabbis to the basic question, "Why do we have the possibility of doing evil?" is that it represents a challenge to man to struggle against the evil, a struggle in which he *can* be victorious. "Sin

3) Deuteronomy, 30:11, 19.
4) Kiddushin, 30b; cf. Berakot, 5a.
5) Genesis Rabbah, 68:18, Genesis, 28:12.

croucheth at the door and unto thee shall be his desire," says the Bible, "but thou shalt rule over it."[6]

But there is a more difficult aspect to the problem of evil than man's struggle with himself concerning his choice of behavior. And this is the more general problem of the very existence of evil and of human suffering in the world. Why should there be suffering? Why do we sometimes see righteous, saintly people suffer, why are they diseased or poverty-stricken? Why must innocent children, newly born, suffer? And, conversely, why do the wicked often prosper? This aspect of the problem is one that has baffled theologians and philosophers throughout the ages. Many have echoed the sentiments of Job, "The world has been turned over into the hands of the wicked"[7] and have felt as he did when he asked, in despair: "Wherefore do the wicked live, become old, yea, wax mighty in power?"[8]

Malaki, one of the Hebrew prophets, also refers to the problem,[9] and the same question reverberates throughout Jewish literature. In the *Yom Kippur* liturgy we read of the martyrdom of the great Rabbis who were put to death by the Romans. And the question is put to God: "Is this the reward for upholding the Torah?" Here are saintly men who devoted all of their lives to the Torah and yet they suffer such tragic deaths. "Does God *avid dina b'lo dina,* pass sentence without justice?"[10] This was the plaintive query of many who were baffled by the problem.

While there is no single answer in Jewish thought to the problem of evil, many of the sages speculated on this subject and formulated views which are worthy of consideration.

The first answer in the Talmud is that punishment is the re-

6) Genesis, 4:7.
7) Job, 9:24.
8) *Ibid.*, 21:7.
9) Malaki, 2:17.
10) Berakot, 5b.

sult of sin. Pain is God's way of chastising man. The Talmud says, "There is no suffering without sin."[11] Sometimes we may not even be conscious of what our sin is, and yet we are made to suffer in order to expiate that sin. The purpose of the suffering that God thus imposes upon us is to make us search and amend our ways, and so do penance and avoid further wrongdoing.[12]

Job is the symbol of the righteous man who suffers. When his friends visit him, they try to convince him that his sufferings must be due to some sins that he committed. But Job keeps repeating that he has not sinned. George Foot Moore, the eminent Christian authority on Judaism, in discussing this scene in the Book of Job, says, "It may be uncharitable when applied by others, but it had its merits when a man was led to examine himself and was led to repentance and amendment."[13] It had its purpose in making man search his ways; in many cases he discovered that he had committed some sin, and he atoned for it through suffering.

This is the answer which the Rabbis gave not only for individual suffering but also for the suffering of exile visited upon the Jewish people. In their prayer services Jews repeat: "It is because of our sins that we have been driven from our land."

But that answer did not satisfy everyone, particularly when they saw that little children or the completely innocent were often afflicted. The Rabbis therefore evolved a new theory, that the righteous man and the innocent child suffer for the "sins of the generation." If many people sin at a given time, as it is said in the Talmud, "the righteous are seized and made to suffer for the sinners. And when there are no righteous, little children are taken from school and are made to suffer because of the sins of others."[14]

11) Shabbat, 55a.
12) Berakot, *ibid.*
13) G. F. Moore, *Judaism*, (Cambridge, Mass., 1927), II, 251.
14) Shabbat, 33b.

When the Rabbis saw that this reply was not fully satisfactory either they formulated still another theory, that "these sufferings and pains are the sufferings of love."[15] They are not really punishments but the trials of Divine love. And one of the Rabbis adds: "Whom the Lord loveth, He chastiseth. This is like the father who chastises a child whom he loves because he wants to encourage him to be better than he is."

But this answer, too, failed to convince many. It simply led some people to say, "Would that God did not love me so much."

Another answer offered was that of *olam haba,* "the future world." This concept of the "future world," which had not been popular in the earlier days of Jewish life, took hold of the Jewish mind and heart and became a great influence because Jews had no other answer to this baffling problem.

The prophets had railed against the sins of nations and had promised the children of Israel rewards and great glory here on earth. But after the destruction of the Temple and the capture of Jerusalem, it seemed as if the very foundation of Jewish life had been broken asunder. The whole problem of reward for suffering and of punishment for evil now begged for a new and more satisfactory answer. Their dream of national glory shattered, Jews had to believe that somewhere, sometime, justice would be done. The heathens would then be punished and the Jews find the reward that was justly theirs. In times of sorrow and stress, the human heart wants to feel that somehow, at some time, justice will bring redress for misery endured. And sorrow and stress were the lot of those generations. They were under the severest political and social oppression.

Jews were thus reassured by the thought that, if man suffers here, he is going to be rewarded in the other world, and if the wicked person is not made to suffer in this life then he is surely going to suffer in the life hereafter. This view provided an an-

15) Berakot, 5a.

swer that sounded plausible, and it gave embodiment to "God's justice." In this way the theory of future reward and punishment evolved and became popular in Jewish thought. The more the Jew suffered, the stronger became his belief in *olam haba*. It was the only recompense he had.

It is true that the medieval Jewish philosophers, Maimonides and others, tried to give philosophical and metaphysical reasons to explain the existence of evil, but their reasoning never gained popular credence. Maimonides identifies God, as Philo of Alexandria did before him, only with the good. If He is the good, evil cannot come from Him. How then account for it? Evil, Maimonides tells us, is the absence of the good, just as darkness is the absence of light. The theory is very intricate, too involved to be interpreted here, and one which, as the historian of Jewish philosophy, Isaac Husik, says, "was extremely unsatisfactory." In fact, after summarizing the theory, Husik concludes: "Maimonides has nothing essentially new to contribute to the solution of the problem."[16] In any case, this theory of "the absence of good" was hardly one to comfort the ordinary human being, and when a later philosopher, Hasdai Crescas, appeared, he taunted Maimonides for his philosophical answers. Crescas repeated what others had said earlier: "There is only one answer and that is *olam haba*, the future world."[17] He felt that no one could be sustained by thinking that evil is not evil, that it is the absence of good, and that God is not responsible for it.

And yet *olam haba* did not answer the problem for many. And the final answer offered by the Rabbis was simply that this is God's way, "it is so decreed by Me."[18] What is decreed by God is futile for man to question. "God so decrees it." Why? We do not know. We must have faith in God and His justice.

16) I. Husik, A History of Mediaeval Jewish Philosophy, (N.Y., 1918), p. 288.
17) Ibid., p. 394.
18) Yoma, 67b.

In this spirit, the prophet Malaki answers the question, "Where is the God of justice?" by saying, "You have wearied the Eternal with your talk. 'How have we wearied Him?' you ask. In that you say.... Where is the God of justice?"[19] You should not even ask the question. That is Malaki's answer. Man has to accept God's judgment, and the Jew has been taught to say unquestioningly, "The Rock, His work is perfect for all His ways are just."[20]

There is a beautiful passage in one of the classic works of the Rabbis which states: "There is a great difference between the heathens and the Jews. The heathens rebel and curse their gods when they are punished, but Israel becomes humble and prays: 'I found trouble and sorrow but then called I upon the name of the Lord.' "[21] The Jew does not rebel; he accepts his judgment and prays to his God.

The brilliant Solomon Schechter, after discussing many of these theories, concludes that there is really no specific view on suffering. Each of the views offered "was simply meant to pacify the mind of the afflicted person so that he should not become despondent and that he should bear his troubles more courageously."[22]

Schechter is correct. None of the theories provides an absolute answer to the problem. They were offered simply as a means to help the sufferers, to ease their suffering, so that they should be able to bear their lot courageously. There is no answer to the problem of evil. It is God's way. "His work is perfect, for all His ways are just." That was essentially the Jewish answer.

There is, however, still a further phase to the problem. While certain evils come from God and we must have faith in God's

19) Malaki, 2:17.
20) Deuteronomy, 32:4.
21) Mekilta, Bachodesh, (ed. Lauterbach) II. p. 277; Psalms, 116:3,4.
22) Solomon Schechter, *Studies in Judaism*, Third Series, (Phila., 1924), pp. 251, 252.

doing, there are other evils and sufferings which come from man, which man himself can conquer. The solution to the first type of evil we must leave to God; the solution to the second, man-made evil, must come from man himself. The evils of war, crime, poverty, ignorance are man-made, not God-made; and they offer a challenge to man to eradicate them.

In the Bible there is a passage which beautifully interprets this thought, against the setting of the battle the Iraelites had to wage against Amalek, one of their great enemies. God urges the Jews: "Remember what Amalek did unto thee." This admonition ends, *emcheh*, "I will blot out the memory of Amalek."[23] The same story is told also in another passage in the Bible, but with the concluding note, *timcheh*, "*You* shall wipe out the memory of Amalek."[24] Amalek is the symbol of wickedness and evil. The subject has two aspects: the eradication of one type of evil we have to leave to God, who in His own time will wipe out that evil; the other type of evil "*thou* must eradicate", man himself has to blot out.

In commenting on this problem, Professor Abraham Heschel says: "We do not know how to solve the problem of *evil*, but we are not exempt from dealing with *evils* in the world which we can eradicate. At the end of days, evil will be conquered by the Holy One. In historic times, now, evils must be conquered one by one."[25]

Let me offer just one further illustration of this thought. In a striking passage in Deuteronomy, God speaks about economic justice and how we should grapple with the problem of the poor. One verse states: "The poor man will never cease to be in the land."[26] There will ever be some who are poor, and therefore we must always open our hand to the needy in

23) Exodus, 17:14.
24) Deuteronomy, 25:19.
25) Abraham Heschel, *God In Search of Man — A Philosophy of Judaism*, (N.Y. 1955), p. 377.
26) Deuteronomy, 15:11.

the land. A few verses earlier, a contrary statement appears: *efes ki lo yiheyeh b'ka evyon,* "However, there shall be no poor among you."[27] The Hebrew text makes clear the apparent contradiction. There shall not be *b'ka, in you,* any cause for your fellow man's poverty!

Even in the ideal state there will always be people who cannot work. But each man must see to it that no poverty should result because of his actions or his wrong or immoral economic way of life. When we are responsible for existing poverty, we are guilty of evil.

In summary, there are aspects of evil which man has the potentiality to remedy. But there are other aspects of evil which he cannot eradicate and which must be left to God. That is the Jewish answer.

In a beautiful passage in one of the ancient classic texts, the Rabbis compare evil to a huge rock, placed on the crossways, over which men stumble as they walk. The king issued a decree to his servants: "Chip it off little by little until the hour comes when I will remove it altogether."[28] Similarly, there are evils which we cannot explain, which God, in His own time, will remove altogether. But there are also evils, part of that "rock," which man can and must chip off little by little so that the road to life's happiness may become easier for all mankind to traverse.

---

27) *Ibid.,* 15:4.
28) Pesikta d'Rav Kahana, (ed. Buber, Lyck, 1868) p. 165a.

Toynbee's
Blind Spot

Discourse delivered at Friday evening service, February 5, 1955, on the publication of the last of the ten volumes of Professor Toynbee's A *Study of History*.

It is seldom that a scientific, historical work has received such wide acclaim as Professor Arnold Toynbee's A *Study of History*. Together with the first six volumes published eight years ago, a single volume summarizing the whole was also issued, thus helping to assure a more popular audience for the historian. And soon this volume did become a best seller and the name of Toynbee familiar to the general public as well as to academics. Now that the final four volumes have appeared, the study has been hailed by many scholars and critics as one of the great contributions to the study of history.

We Jews have a particular interest in this study. Far from ignoring the Jew, Toynbee interprets the Jew and his history and does so in a way that calls for an answer and an analysis. Let there be no doubt about it, Toynbee is one of the intellectual giants of our age. His knowledge, revealed in these ten volumes, is phenomenal. He seems to have mastered, with an encyclopedic sweep, many phases of human history, and he gives us not only the facts of history but also an interpretation. He is primarily the philosopher of history, and that is what the true historian should be. It is interesting to note that the ancient Rabbis had the same concept of history. Discussing the historical books of the Bible, they say: *lo nitnah divre hayamin ela l'hidaresh*, "historical facts were given only to be interpreted."[1]

1) Ruth Rabbah, 2:1.

The trouble with Toynbee's interpretations, however, is that when he analyzes and interprets the history of most civilizations, he usually does so clearly, and endeavors to be objective, but when he discusses the history of the Jews, a dark curtain obstructs his vision.

When I read his passages dealing with the Jew and his role in history, past and present, I recalled a familiar character, Balaam, portrayed for us in the Bible and in the commentaries of the Rabbis. You recall that Balak, king of Moab, summoned Balaam to hurl his incantations against the Israelites and thus to destroy them.[2] Balaam, according to the Rabbis, was not an ordinary man; they tell us he was the greatest prophet and the outstanding sage of all the gentile nations of his day. He had acquired a position in the non-Jewish world as exalted as that of Moses among the Jews.[3] However, he suffered from a serious disability, according to the sages: *Bilaam suma b'achat m'eynav haya*, "Balaam was blind in one eye."[4] Another Talmudic passage states, *chiger b'raglo achat haya*, "Balaam was crippled in one foot."[5] These are strange and interesting statements. We could well understand a tradition telling us that Balaam was blind or that he was crippled. Why should the sages emphasize that he was blind only in one eye and crippled only in one foot? But it is just this fact that they wanted to emphasize for us. When Balaam scanned the life of the other nations and prophesied about their fate, he looked clearly with his seeing eye, and approached their problems with the firm step of his good foot; thus he deservedly won a reputation as his people's greatest seer. It was only when he studied the Jew's life and tried to look into the Jew's future that he used his blind eye and treaded with his crippled foot.

With all due respect to Professor Toynbee, we may truth-

2) Numbers, ch. 22-24.
3) Baba Bathra, 15b; Numbers Rabbah, 20:1.
4) Sanhedrin, 105a.
5) Sotah, 10a.

fully say that the Rabbinic description of Balaam equally applies to him. He has a penetrating eye when he views the life of all other peoples and civilizations; it is with remarkable objectivity that he analyzes in the latter volumes the tragedy of the modern nations, the democratic as well as the communist, their inherent faults and weaknesses, their wanton nationalism and national jealousies, their surrender of spiritual values, their idealization of material power and success. He is firm and bold in his approach to modern Christianity. Devout Christian that he is, he nevertheless sees clearly and excoriates the current vulgarization of many of the churches and their leaders. It is only in his discussion of the Jew, of the Jew's contribution to civilization, the modern problems of the Jew, that his vision is blinded and his approach crippled.

In his work, Toynbee studies twenty-one civilizations that have developed throughout the ages, a number of which have already vanished. History is the story of their rise and their fall. Among the twenty-one enumerated, he finds no place for the Jewish civilization. There *is* a leading civilization which arose in the Mediterranean region, according to Toynbee, but that is the Syriac, not the Jewish, civilization. The Israelite nation is nothing more than a remnant of the Syriac civilization, and this, despite the uniqueness of the Israelite religion and the great difference between its contributions and those of the Syriac civilization. Because the early Israelites settled in the part of Canaan that was later known as Syria, Toynbee makes them a part of the Syriac civilization.

Toynbee himself is forced to admit that, "In a period of their history which began in the infancy of the Syriac civilization, and which culminated in the age of the Prophets, the people of Israel and Judea raised themselves, head and shoulders above the Syriac peoples round about, by rising to a monotheistic conception of religion." However, in another section, speaking of the Syriac discovery of the alphabet and the Phoenician discovery of the Atlantic ocean, he says: "But

these physical discoveries are surpassed by the spiritual dis-
covery of monotheism, and that was the feat of a Syriac community, stranded in the hill country of Ephraim and Judah."
Mind you, he does recognize the superiority of this spiritual
discovery, monotheism, but he speaks of it as "the feat of a
Syriac community," not the feat of the Israelite community.
The latter, for him, is nothing more than a remnant of the
Syriac civilization. It sounds unbelievable, but Toynbee even
robs the Jew of his Bible, the Jew's greatest gift to the world!
He is fascinated by a Biblical passage (I Kings III) which tells
of young Solomon's request of God: "Give thy servant an understanding heart, that I may discern between good and evil,"
but he refers to it as a Syriac fable, carefully refraining from
crediting this passage to the Jew.

If you ask how Toynbee reconciles his minimizing, even his
ignoring, the Israelite civilization, with his admitted recognition of the greatness and the superiority of monotheism and
the genius of the prophets, his answer is that "they had indeed
been gifted with unparalleled spiritual insight," but "it was a
momentary spiritual eminence" that they had achieved. It was
only for a moment, nothing more, that the Jew rose to eminence; it was an accident, not the result of Jewish genius, civilization, or history that accounted for this "unparalleled spiritual insight." It is odd especially in the terms of Toynbee's
own historical schemes that something "unparalleled" should
arise accidently in an insignificant environment. But, philosopher and historian that Toynbee is, he seems to forget that
even if this statement were true, a contribution of only a solitary moment may be so great as to influence all the ages to
follow.

Worst of all is his treatment of the Jew after the destruction
of the second temple and the Jew's exile from his ancient land.
Judaism, to him ceased with that event to function as a vital
force. He looks upon Judaism throughout these nineteen centuries as "a petrified religion, which has lost its message to

mankind and has hardened into a fossil of the extinct Syrian society." Again and again he refers to the Jew and to Judaism as an extinct society which survives only as a fossil. To such an extent have we disappeared as a world influence that when he speaks of the future and pleads for a synthesis of what is best in the world's great religions of today, he names "Christianity, Mohammedanism, Buddhism, and Confucianism," but fails to include Judaism.

How can one account for such an egregious misinterpretation of Jewish history, such contempt for Judaism's contributions to world civilization? The answer is quite simple, and Toynbee himself gives us a clue. He is a pious Christian and he cannot forgive the Jews for what he regards as their great sin. "They had indeed been gifted with unparalleled spiritual insight... but they rejected the still greater treasure which God offered them in the coming of Jesus of Nazareth.... He was rejected by the Judean leaders of the Jewry of his own age. Thereby Judaism not only stultified its past, but forfeited its future." Here is the answer. Toynbee adheres to the original, classic Christian theology, that with the appearance of Christianity Judaism ceased to exist, that the Church henceforth was the true Israel. What you see of the Jew is only a ghost, and of Judaism only a fossil of a petrified religion.

Now we can understand Toynbee's strong opposition to the Jewish revival of our day. He laughs at the Jew's attempt to rebuild his homeland in Palestine. The "Zionist Jews suffer from archaism," he tells us. "They want to go back to their childhood!" He even ridicules the Jew's attempt to revive the Hebrew language as a living spoken tongue. Hebrew has been dead, he tells us, for the last 2,300 years. It is hardly necessary to dispute this misstatement of fact which Toynbee, as a historian, should have realized. The Hebrew language was never dead. Throughout the ages Hebrew was the language used by scholar, sage and writer. It was the language taught to students young and old. Toynbee could have seen, if he had not looked

with the blind eye, how Hebrew has become revitalized, with a
rich literature, not only in the new Israel but also among tens
of thousands of Jews elsewhere throughout the world. Even today he is bitter against the Jewish State. We can well understand this bitterness, for during the last world war Toynbee
had worked under the late Ernest Bevin, British Foreign Minister, the arch antagonist of Israel, and it is evident that even
a great mind can become warped through contact with such
prejudice.

But the real reason for Toynbee's opposition to Israel is
again to be found in his fundamentalist Christian theology.
For according to early Christian teaching, the Jew was to be
the eternal wanderer until he recognized his national sin and
accepted the Christian redeemer. Only then could the restoration of the Jew in Zion be fulfilled. It is interesting to observe
that while Toynbee denounces the "Zionist Jews," he has high
praise for *Agudat Yisrael,* the ultra-orthodox group in Jewry, which refuses to hasten God's ways "through an impious
usurpation of God's prerogative by human hands of bringing
about the restoration." Had Toynbee been up to date, he
would have known that even the *Agudat Yisrael* has under-
gone a change of heart, and that the great majority of this
group has now recognized the State of Israel and is working
for its growth and welfare.

But that is Toynbee's belief, that the Jew has usurped God's
prerogative in restoring his national life. He would have us remain in the ghettoes of the nations, still holding the wandering staff in our hands. He does not like the new Jew that Israel
has produced. "In the last thirty years," he writes, "the Zioni-
ist pioneers in Palestine duly achieved this most incredible
tour de force by minting a fresh type of Jew in whom the child
of the diaspora is no longer recognizable." This is what we are
proud of, that the Jew in Israel stands erect, his back no longer
bent. He faces the world proud of his heritage and his achievements. We glory in the fact that in the new Israel we behold

the answer to our age-long prayer, the fulfillment of the prophet's promise that God will lead us to our land *kommemiyut*, standing erect and upright. Toynbee would prefer to see us a fossil of a dead civilization, providing proof of the old Christian doctrine.

One of Toynbee's most interesting theories explains why certain civilizations have died. They disappear, according to him, not because of attacks from outside enemies, but because of their failure to respond to new challenges of their time. "Through challenge and response to further challenge, this is the essence of being alive," he tells us. By that very definition, Toynbee should have glorified the Jew. For what is the Jew's history but a constant response to challenges, arising in every age and in every land? What is Zionism if not a response to an inward challenge and a challenge from the nations of the world? His very definition proves most eloquently that the Jew and the Jewish civilization are very much alive, the living evidence of the truth of the Psalmist's words: "I shall not die, but live, and declare the works of God!"[6]

How then are we to interpret Toynbee himself? He is, indeed, no anti-Semite in the ordinary meaning of that term. He denounces in strongest terms Hitler's cruelties against the Jews, and I am certain that he would defend the Jew everywhere against physical oppression. I think, however, that we may consider him guilty of what the brilliant Solomon Schechter characterized as the "higher anti-Semitism." He would not hurt the body of the Jew, but he would rob him of his soul, his spiritual self. The Rabbis of the Talmud, in their further portrayal of Balaam, the ancient prophet of the gentile world, make an interesting play on his name, *Bilaam, bala am*, "he wanted to swallow, to annihilate, the people of Israel."[7] Professor Toynbee would like to consume the life-giving soul and

6) Psalms, 118:17
7) Sanhedrin, 105a.

spirit of the Jew, to render the significance of his history life-
less, to leave him possessor of a remnant of a petrified religion.

As brilliant as his study is when he considers the achievements of other civilizations, it is blind and unjust when he attempts to interpret Judaism. It is the distinction of the Jew
that he responded in glorious fashion to the challenges of the
Balaams of every age. He will respond, I am confident, in
equally glorious fashion to the challenge of the Balaam of our
day. He will work and strive and sacrifice to rebuild his own life
everywhere, and the life of his people in their old-new land,
so that he may continue to contribute his blessed spiritual
and cultural gifts to the enhancement of world civilization.

You may recall the conclusion of the Biblical story of the
ancient Balaam. He came to curse Israel, but instead was
forced to bless her. I have the faith and the confidence that
though Professor Toynbee came to ridicule and to denounce
Israel's attempt to revitalize his national and spiritual life,
that though he would have the world believe the Jew is no more
than a fossil and Judaism a petrified religion, the day will yet
come and soon, when Professor Toynbee will see with two clear
eyes the flowering of a great and blessed Jewish civilization on
Zion's heights and in many of the lands of the Diaspora; and
when he, too, like Balaam of old, will proclaim: "How beautiful are thy tents, O Jacob, thy tabernacles, O Israel!"[8]

EPILOGUE

Professor Toynbee has recently published another volume,
Reconsiderations (1961), in which he modifies slightly some
of his strictures on the Jews and Judaism; but in the main the
criticism in this discourse are still valid and even more necessary. For in the new volume Toynbee urges the renunciation
by the diaspora Jews of their "communal identity" and their

8) Numbers, 24:5.

repudiation of the Torah, so that they may be free to convert mankind to the religion of the Prophets. This proposal reminds us of the well-known quip of Israel Zangwill, in answer to those who offered the Jew similar advice in order to hasten the day when the "wolf shall dwell with the lamb:" "That day would come, but the lamb would be inside the wolf!" Dr. Toynbee has also contributed an article to the *Jewish Quarterly Review* (July, 1961), attacking the legal claim of the Jews to Palestine. A well-written, scholarly reply by Professor Solomon Zeitlin, of Dropsie College, appearing in the same issue of the *Review*, clearly proves that Toynbee's article consists of *"ex cathedra* statements, punctuated with half truths and inspired with the eloquence of bias and prejudice."

The Youthful President Kennedy and The Youthfulness of the Biblical Joseph

Preached on Sabbath *Beshalach*, January 28, 1961, on the occasion of the 60th anniversary of the *Bar Mitzvah* of the Rabbi. This sermon was printed in the U.S. Congressional Record, April 26, 1961, in conjunction with remarks by Hon. Edna F. Kelly, of Brooklyn, N.Y., member of the House of Representatives.

It is now some time since the presidential election; most of us saw on television or read in the newspapers of the impressive inauguration of our new President. Whether we are Republicans or Democrats, all of us, in the true American spirit, accept the verdict of the electorate and join in the fervent prayer that Heaven's blessings may accompany President Kennedy in all his paths of duty, and that he may succeed in strengthening the role of genuine democracy in our land and in bringing the world nearer to the goals of universal peace and human brotherhood.

It is the accepted role of the clergyman not to take an active part in political campaigns unless a great moral issue is at stake. Throughout my ministry I have adhered to this rule. Now, however, that the election is over, it is not out of place for a clergyman to comment on various aspects of the campaign. It is in this spirit that I would like to offer my views on the subject this Sabbath morning.

One of the things that struck me as strange in the recent campaign was the emphasis which the Republican leaders had placed upon Senator Kennedy's youth. I recall reading in the press that at the first meeting of the Republican Strategy Committee, immediately following the nominating conventions,

118

it was unanimously decided to issue a directive to all Republican speakers that they should never refer to the Democratic nominee as Senator Kennedy but always as the *young* or *youthful* Senator Kennedy, implying of course that youth meant immaturity, inexperience, naiveté.

That a man of 43 should be regarded as a youth was something that I could not comprehend. In the Jewish tradition, a lad of 13 is regarded as already mature enough for the performance of religious duties. At 18, according to the Rabbis, he is ready to marry and to assume the responsibilities of family life. At 30, a man is deemed to reach the height of physical vigor; and at 40, to attain full strength of mind and understanding.[1] Indeed, in an interesting passage in our ancient Rabbinic literature, there is a discussion on this very theme: "Unto what age can a man be called a *naar*, a youth? Rabbi Akiba said: up to the age of 30; Rabbi Meir said: up to 25; and Rabbi Samuel said: they are both wrong, only up to 20 years of age."[2] To the Jewish mind it would be absolutely incomprehensible to speak of a man of 43 as young or as a youth.

In any case, we might ask what is wrong or objectionable in being young? It seems to me, as one who has already reached the age of the hoary head, that youth is one of man's greatest blessings and that youth offers a person great, creative opportunities. Lord Beaconsfield, from the richness of his experience, cried out: "We must be young to do great things!" And William Hazlitt, the celebrated British critic, gave as his judgment that "almost everything great has been achieved by youth!" Allowing for exaggeration in these statements, we certainly cannot agree that being young in itself is synonymous with immaturity or makes one unfit for leadership. Furthermore, there is a difference of only 3 or 4 years between the

1) Abot, 5:24.
2) Yalkut Shimoni, Proverbs, 1:4.

ages of Kennedy and Nixon; and if at 43 one is young, and at
46 or 47 one is fully grown, the question arises: which year is
the dividing line between youth and ripened age?

It is interesting to note that in this Sabbath's Scriptural
reading there is a reference to the great Biblical character,
Joseph. Four weeks ago we concluded the story of his dramatic
life. Since then, we have been reading the story of the bondage
of the Israelites in Egypt, and today's Scriptural portion describes the exodus from Egypt and the passage of the Israelites through the Red Sea. But in the midst of today's verses
we are again reminded of Joseph: "And Moses took the bones
of Joseph with him."[3]

Let us turn for a moment to the early phase of Joseph's
life. You recall the story: how he is imprisoned in Egypt, how,
while a prisoner, he correctly interprets the dreams of Pharaoh's butler and baker. And now Pharaoh dreams a dream
which no one can interpret for him. The butler reminds himself of his own dream while imprisoned and how Joseph's interpretation was fulfilled. He had forgotten his promise to
Joseph that he would remember him and speak well of him to
the Egyptian authorities; but now the opportunity is his to
serve his master and to win his favor. And so he approaches
Pharaoh and tells him of his own experience: "And there was
with us a *naar ivri*, a Hebrew youth who interpreted for us our
dreams."[4]

The Rabbis were astonished that the butler had referred to
Joseph as *naar*, a youth. The Bible itself tells us that he was
30 years old when he stood before Pharaoh[5], and how can one
speak of a man of 30 as a *naar*? But the Rabbis have a ready
answer: the butler referred to him in a derogatory sense,
k'shoteh, a foolish, immature, inexperienced lad, *v'en raui*

3) Exodus, 13:19.
4) Genesis, 41:12.
5) *Ibid.*, 41:46.

ligdulah, unfit for position of greatness or leadership.[6]

Pharaoh, however, at his first meeting with Joseph, immediately recognized his greatness, and appointed him to the high position of vice-ruler of the realm. And the masses of Egypt also recognized his qualities of leadership, "and they called unto him *avrek*," a strange word, which the Rabbis translated as *av b'chakmah v'rak b'shanim*, "patriarch in wisdom and youthful in years!"[7] It was this combination possessed by Joseph, maturity in wisdom, youthfulness, not so much in years, but, as one commentator translates *rak b'tiveo*, "in his nature," in spirit, which captivated the minds of the ruler and the masses of Egypt![8]

I have the feeling that what helped President Kennedy more than anything else was that millions of our citizens recognized in him this remarkable combination of *av b'chakmah*, rich maturity in wisdom, and *rak b'shanim*, a youthfulness in his very nature and spirit. One may be old in years and yet be blessed with such youthfulness in spirit. Moses, the Bible tells us, was 80 years old when he undertook the difficult task of delivering his people from their Egyptian bondage.[9] In our own day, we see Ben Gurion, at 74, yet blessed with the spirit of youth in directing the affairs of state in Israel.

As a matter of fact, the Bible often uses the term *naar* not in the sense of youth but in that of *youthfulness*, and thus refers to a number of the ancient heroes as *naar*, though they were advanced in years. "And Joshua, his servant, *naar*," yet the Rabbis tell us that he was then 42 years of age.[10] David speaks of "my son Solomon *naar*," again the Rabbis tell us he too was then 42 years old.[11] Speaking of the spies whom

6) Rashi, *ibid.*, 41:12.
7) Genesis, 41:43; Rashi, *ibid.*
8) Malbim, 1 Chronicles, 22:5.
9) Exodus, 7:7.
10) *Ibid.*, 33:11; Rashi, 1 Chron., 22:5.
11) Rashi, *ibid.*

Joshua sent to investigate the city of Jericho, the Rabbis tell us that they were Caleb and Pinchas, and that Caleb was then 78 years old.[12] Yet the Bible speaks of them as *naarim*, youths, and the Rabbis continue their comment: "The Bible calls them youths, *shehayu zerizim k'naarim*, because they were as energetic, as enthusiastic, as zealous as young men."[13] The Prophet Hosea, speaking of God's love for Israel, tells us: *ki naar Yisrael, v'ohavehu*, usually translated, "When Israel was a youth, I loved him."[14] I think the meaning of the verse is: "*Because* Israel is *youthful*, I loved him."

Though Israel is among the oldest of the world's peoples, it is today again revealing its spirit of youthfulness, its power of creativity in every field of human endeavor.

And this is what America, as well as the world at large, craves: the spirit which youth typifies, vigor, enthusiasm, adventure, and the daring to translate into action the ripe wisdom and experience which a leader may possess. Such is the quality of leadership which the American people have recognized in President Kennedy, and which has won their hearts.

And now we can better understand the deeper meaning of our text in this Sabbath's Scriptural lesson: "And Moses took the bones of Joseph with him."[15] The Rabbis were puzzled by this verse: *mai immo*, they ask, "Why did Moses have to carry the bones of Joseph *with him*?"[16] Could he not have assigned other Jews to perform that task? Many are the interpretations which the sages offer. I think the answer is simple. Moses was quite old in years at the time, past 80 years of age. But he held on to the body of Joseph as a constant inspiration, as a challenge to try to retain the spirit of youthfulness which Joseph had typified. Moses realized that once that spirit of

12) Zevachim, 118b; cf. Joshua, 14:7, 10; Numbers Rabbah, 16:1.
13) Rashi, Joshua, 6:23.
14) Hosea, 11:1.
15) Exodus, 13:19.
16) Nazir, 45a.

youthfulness departed from him his power of leadership would also depart!

If I may be permitted, I should like to add a personal word. This Sabbath has a special significance for me: it is my *Bar Mitzvah* Sabbath. Many years have passed since that eventful day in my life, sixty to be exact. I realize that I have long passed the stage of *naar*, of youth. I have already passed the stages of *ziknah* and *sevah*, by which the Rabbis designate one's 60th and 70th years.[17] But, like Moses, I, too, symbolically speaking, want to cling to the bones of Joseph and to retain his spirit of *naarut*, of youthfulness, and to be *zariz k'naar*, to retain the zeal, the vigor, the enthusiasm of youth, so for years to come you may be able to say: *ki naar Yisrael*, for Israel is still young in spirit, and therefore I may continue to have your regard and your esteem.

And thus we offer a fervent prayer this Sabbath to our Heavenly Father, first in behalf of our new President, that he may ever be blessed with the gifts of *av b'chakmah*, maturity in wisdom, and of *rak b'shanim*, the spirit of youthfulness in years. And for myself and for all the older men and women in our congregation, I pray that we may be enabled to be *zerizim k'naarim*, active, vigorous, energetic like the young, so that we may continue to serve our faith, our people, our beloved America, and all mankind.

17 Abot, 5:24.

"Like a Ray of Sunshine"

Radio address over Station WOR,
November 16, 1945.

I should like to interpret for you a familiar scene which is portrayed for us in the pages of our Bible. The patriarch Abraham is pictured sitting at the door of his tent *k'chom hayom*, "in the heat of the day."[1] He is gazing about, looking for strangers, to whom he may offer a welcome to his home. The story is surely familiar to you of how, raising his eyes, he beholds three men standing in the distance. He runs toward them and pleads with them: "Do not pass by your servant . . . have a little water brought to wash your feet; then lie down under the tree till I fetch a bite of food to refresh you; after that you can go on!"[2] This is one of the most beautiful descriptions of human kindness and sympathy to be found in all the world's literature.

May I pause, in particular, to interpret the special, descriptive phrase which the Bible adds in the beginning of this story: Abraham was sitting at the door of his tent "in the heat of the day." The original Hebrew text says: *"k'chom hayom."* Literally, these words do not mean *"in* the heat of the day;" *k'chom hayom* really means *"like* the warmth of day!" What a new insight into the entire picture these words offer us! Abraham was sitting there, *like the warmth of noonday,* or to put it in modern phraseology, he was sitting at the door of his tent like a ray of sunshine to those who were tired, weary, hungry, despairing, to those who felt the icy chill of loneliness, who

1) Genesis, 18:1.
2) *Ibid.,* v. 3-5.

saw only darkness surrounding them. Yea, that is the way he must have appeared to these three forlorn sun-beaten strangers, to whom he offered such a hearty, brotherly welcome to the shelter of his home.

There are such people, fortunately, who stand out *k'chom hayom*, "like the warmth of noonday," in this cold, dreary world of ours. There is kindness in every word that comes from their lips; there is sympathetic warmth in their every act. You feel drawn to them by the love that shines from their eyes. They may be strangers to you, but somehow you feel the closeness of brothers in their presence. The ancient Rabbis emphasize this thought again and again in our classic literature. There are men, they tell us, who, when they come into your presence, "bring the fragrance of the Garden of Eden with them." There are others, on the other hand, who, when they appear before you, "seem to bear the odor of *Gehenna*, of Hell, itself."[3]

Abraham, the founder of monotheism and the father of the people of Israel, is thus pictured as exemplifying in life what religion should mean to each and every one of us. Religion is that Divine force which should make its adherents stand out as rays of sunshine, bringing the warmth of brotherhood and kindness to every man, especially to those who need that warmth in the icy path of hunger and loneliness which they are forced to tread.

It is interesting to see how the ancient Rabbis elaborated upon this Biblical picture. These three strangers, according to the Bible story, were in reality angels disguised as men. But see! They did not appear to Abraham as members of his own tribe or as followers of his own faith. On the contrary, they appeared as total strangers. Our sages say that one was disguised as a Saracean, one as a Nabataean, and one as an Arabian.[4]

3) *Cf.* Genesis Rabbah, 65:18.
4) *Ibid.*, 48:9.

That did not matter to Abraham, he was like a ray of sunshine to every man, regardless of nationality or faith, because his heart radiated with warmth, with love and with brotherliness to all humanity.

Oh, how the world needs such rays of human sunshine. When we gaze across the ocean to foreign lands or even examine our own, and behold the misery of millions of persons, hopeless because of the bleakness and the darkness which encompass them, we see the need for this interpretation of religion, which would make of all of us living rays of sunshine.

Let us then translate this message of religion in our daily lives. In all our relationships with our fellow men — at home or abroad — let us endeavor to appear to them *k'chom hayom*, like rays of sunshine, and we shall thus help to make of this world a better, happier, kindlier, nobler world than we know today.

Walls of Hatred From the Right and From the Left

Preached on the concluding day of Passover,
April 26, 1962.

The initial days of the Passover festival recall the first act in the drama of Israel's emancipation from bondage in Egypt. They tell of the sufferings of our people while enslaved, of the Divine call to Moses to become their deliverer, of Pharaoh's capitulation to God's command to let His people go free. These concluding days of the festival relate the second act of this drama, how Pharaoh changed his mind, regretting his action, and how he and his army pursued the Israelites in an attempt to enslave them again. The Israelites were now in panic. They saw the Egyptians approaching, but could go no farther in their flight, they were facing the waters of the Red Sea.

You remember the conclusion of the drama, how God said to Moses: "Speak unto the children of Israel, that they go forward";[1] how the waters of the sea were divided; "and the children of Israel went into the midst of the sea upon the dry ground, and the waters were a *chomah*, a wall, unto them, *miminam umismolam*, on their right hand and on their left."[2] The Israelites were saved, and while the Egyptians were pursuing them in the same dry path, the sea returned to its strength, and covered the chariots and the horsemen, even all the host of Pharaoh that went in after them into the sea."[3] A few

1) Exodus, 14:15.
2) *Ibid.*, v. 22.
3) *Ibid.*, v. 28.

127

verses later, the Bible repeats what happened: "And the children of Israel walked upon dry land in the midst of the sea;
and the waters were a wall unto them on their right hand and
on their left."[4]

This reiteration is very strange. The Bible is sparing in its
use of words, and does not repeat just for the sake of repetition. The Rabbis, however, noticed in these sentences a difference in the spelling of the Hebrew word for "wall." In the
first, the word *chomah* is spelled the correct way, including the
letter *vav*; in the second, the word *chomah* omits the *vav*.
This variation led them to make this interesting comment,
"In the second sentence, read not *chomah, wall,* but *chemah,
fury, hatred, wrath.*"[5]

Here is a keen insight into the revelations of the Bible. The
first account refers to the incident that happened when Israel
fled from the Egyptians. The second account, I believe, is a
prophetic portrayal of what was to face the Jews in the years
ahead. They would have to make their way through life "upon
dry ground in the midst of the sea, and the waters shall be
walls of *chemah*, of fury unto them on their right hand and
on their left." How true this prediction has been! Throughout
their tragic history, especially in the last two thousand years,
the march of the Jews through life has been on a narrow, dry
path in the midst of a raging sea, with walls of *chemah*, hatred and rage, on their right and on their left!

But there is still a deeper thought inherent in this text. The
words *miminam umismolam* are not literally translated in
our English versions, neither in the above translation given in
the old Jewish Publication Society's edition of the Bible, nor
in James Moffatt's *New Translation*, which renders the expression "forming a wall to right and left." If the text, however, meant to say "*on* their right and *on* their left," the He-

4) *Ibid.*, v. 29.
5) Mekilta (ed. Lauterbach), Vol. 1, p. 247.

brew expression would have to be *liminam v'lismolam*. What the words say literally is: *"from* their right and *from* their left", an expression giving rise to a new insight.

The words "right" and "left" are quite significant. In modern times they are a definite terminology commonly used in the fields of politics, economics, and sociology. The "leftists" represent the radicals in these fields, from so-called liberals to revolutionaries. The "rightists" represent the conservatives in these fields, from the standpatters to the reactionaries. And while neither the Bible nor the ancient sages had the contemporary usage of these terms in mind, we may — with homiletic license — apply the comment to a modern interpretation.

Jewish experience throughout the ages and in every land has taught us that anti-Semitism can often be expected *from the right* — from the rightists — whether in the sphere of religion or economics or politics. Alas, the walls of fury and rage against the Jew usually came *miminam*, from the right. It is not difficult to discern a reason for such hatred. Judaism is a forward-looking religion and civilization, liberal and progressive in its spirit and philosophy. It opposes human bondage whether it be in economic, political, or social life. It envisions an age of universal and genuine peace, brotherhood and freedom blessing the life of all mankind. The rightists who look askance at such aims and ideals will, of course, form walls of hatred against the Jew.

We should, however, have the right to expect no such walls of hatred coming "from the left." The Jews have generally been on the side of liberalism. Although they have been opposed to that extreme type of leftist ideology which sanctions cruel and tyrannous methods to achieve its aims, we should think that anti-Semitism would be abhorrent even to the extreme leftists. But the prophetic warning in our Biblical text is wiser. Alas, that is the tragedy history reveals, *chemah*, fury against the Jews comes also *mismolam*, from the left.

Several years ago an interesting study on the subject appeared in a scholarly journal: "Was Karl Marx an Anti-Semite?"[6] The question posed seems unbelievable. Marx, the father of Socialism, looked upon by many as the modern Messiah to usher in an era of happiness for all men by revolutionizing the world's economic system, how could he possibly be swayed by a fury of hatred against the Jew? And yet this writer, quoting from Marx's many articles and letters, gives definite proof of his raging bias and prejudice against the Jew! Yea, it is difficult to explain, but history gives ample proof of this *chemah* that came from the hearts of those on the left.

Another article, also in a scholarly journal,[7] tells us what happened after the French Revolution, which proclaimed to the world the ideals of Liberty, Fraternity, Equality. Soon after the revolution, when the question was raised in the French Assembly whether to grant French Jews the right to vote and to hold political office, the prophetic warning in the Bible again proved true. It could naturally have been expected that opposition would come *miminam*, from the right. The Royalists,

---

6) E. Silberner, *Historia Judaica*, Vol. XI no. 1 (April, 1949). See also S. F. Bloom, "Karl Marx and the Jews", *Jewish Social Studies*, Vol. IV, no. 1 (Jan., 1942). See also a recent publication: A *World Without Jews*, by Karl Marx, translated, with an Introduction by Dagobert D. Runes.

7) Z. Szajkowski, "Socialist Anti-Semites in France", *Jewish Social Studies*, Vol. IX (1947). See also Edmund Silberner, "Anti Jewish Trends in French Revolutionary Syndicalism", *Ibid.*, Vol. XV, no. 3-4 (1953) — "French Revolutionary Syndicalism offers a good example of how anti-Semitism can penetrate even into the most radical leftist circles" (p. 195).

The historian Oscar Handlin, in an article dealing with this very theme, shows that the emergence of ideological anti-Semitism in the United States, contrary to general opinion, was due to the growth of certain forms of "grass-roots" radicalism in the 90's. "And significantly," he writes, "the mass of decent folk who joined the Klan and read the *Dearborn Independent* came from areas that had in the 1890's been strongly moved by radicalism." "How U.S. Anti-Semitism Really Began," *Commentary*, (June, 1951).

the reactionaries in church and politics were loud and furious in fighting to defeat the proposals. The French Jew knew that opposition would come from these sources. But how disappointed he was that the same opposition came also *mismolam*, from the left! Giving new rationalizations for their stand, many of these leftists joined the rightists in *chemah* to the Jew.

And today, one of the baffling mysteries is the attitude of the Russian government towards the Jew in the Soviet Union. Here is a government representing the extreme left, that claims to have ushered in an era of equality for all its inhabitants; and yet, look at the special, oppressive measures it has adopted to stifle the religious and cultural life of the Jew. Look, too, at its inexplicable hatred toward the State of Israel, the only exponent of genuine freedom and democracy in the Near East, and at its close alignment with the Arab States, most of which are under autocratic rule, keeping the masses in ignorance, poverty, and oppression. Who could have foretold such close affinity between the supreme exemplar of the leftist philosophy and the egregious exponent of the rightist in their united desire to destroy Israel! How truly the words of the Psalmist apply to this union of Russia and the Arab States towards reborn Israel: "They hold crafty converse against Thy people. . . . They have said: 'Come, and let us cut them off from being a nation; that the name of Israel may be no more in remembrance.' For they have consulted together with one consent; against Thee do they make a covenant; the tents of Edom and the Ishmaelites."[8] Yea, Russia, the real *Edom*, descendant of Esau, the true Red, aligned with the offspring of Ishmael, in a covenant to cut Israel off from being a nation!

How can we explain this phenomenon? The answer, I believe, is simple. These leftists concentrate on their economic interpretation of history, as if man himself will be transformed

8) Psalms, 83:4, 5.

if the economic system alone be changed. Judaism saw more
deeply into the situation of the world and man's life. The evils
inherent in the present economic system of many parts of the
world must be remedied. The prophets of Israel pleaded for
economic reform. They denounced the unbridled power and
misuse of wealth in their day. But they realized that such reform alone was not enough; they insisted that there had to be
a change in man's heart if freedom, tolerance, and genuine
brotherhood were ever to bless the life of man: "A new heart
will I give you, and a new spirit will I put within you, and I will
take away the heart of stone out of you, and I will give you a
heart of flesh."[9]

Even if Communism offered the final economic solution,
and it does not seem to do even that — it would still not be
adequate to do away with the hatred that fills men's hearts. To
usher in the Messianic era man needs a new heart that shall
beat with sympathy towards all men, a new spirit that shall
evince the recognition that all men are brothers. Until that
transformation of heart and spirit is achieved, economic improvement, though offering slight and temporary relief, is
worthless as far as the long-range security and peace of man is
concerned.

And this failure to see the insufficiency of the Marxist philosophy, alas, was the tragic mistake of many of our own young
people and intellectuals, who formerly hailed the slogans with
which the Russian revolutionaries heralded the salvation of
the world and of the Jew. How disillusioned they are today!
As long as we see *chemah*, walls of hatred, toward the Jew from
these exponents of the left, we must recognize that they are
false prophets and false messiahs who can only bemuse and
lead astray the minds of men.

We Jews must take to heart this Biblical warning, that our
salvation will not come either from the rightists or the leftists.

9) Ezekiel, 36:26.

Let us not be swayed by sweet words emanating from either camp. Paraphrasing the words of the Psalmist, we may truly say: "Put not your trust in so-called princes, nor in the son of man in whom there is no help; his momentary good spirit departs and he returns to his earthly self; on that day his good thoughts depart."[10]

Our solution is given in the Biblical story: "Speak to the children of Israel that they go forward!" Even though we are faced by walls of *chemah* from the right and left, and even though we have to traverse a narrow, dry path in the midst of a raging sea of hate, we have no other course to take but to go forward, clinging to our ideals, to our genuine Messianic hopes.

Commenting upon the very scene which this festival recalls, the Rabbis ask: "And what caused them to be saved *miminam umismolam*, from their right and from their left?" *Torah utfillah*, "Their devotion to Torah, the embodiment of the priceless teachings of their faith, and the inspiration which they drew from their prayers, their communion with God."[11] These same qualities or forces which preserved us in the past will continue to give us strength and hope until the day dawns when men transform their hearts of stone into hearts of flesh, when *chemah*, hatred, will be removed from all hearts and minds, and when every man will be able to sit under his own vine and figtree with no one to make him afraid!"[12]

10) Cf. Psalms, 146:3, 4.
11) Mekilta, vol. 1, p. 247.
12) Cf. Micah, 4:4.

The Miracle of Reborn Israel

Address delivered, January 29, 1961, at Dinner of the
Brooklyn Division of the Jewish National Fund, marking
the establishment of a Foresters' Village in the Freedom
Forest in Israel, in honor of the fiftieth anniversary of my
Rabbinate in Brooklyn.

I bring to you greetings from our brethren in the new-born
State of Israel, who appreciate the important role that American Jewry has played in the historic drama of the establishment of the State, and whose plea to you is: Continue to "seek
the peace of Jerusalem!"[1] Would that I were able to portray to
you in adequate detail the great miracle that we beheld in that
old-new land and among its people. I can best summarize it
in the words with which the Rabbis described the Temple service in ancient days: "Happy and fortunate is the eye that has
seen all this."

I can perhaps appreciate the greatness of this miracle much
more than the average tourist, for this was our third visit to
this historic land. We first visited it in 1925, when, as a dele-
gate of the United Synagogue of America, the New York
Board of Rabbis, and our own Brooklyn Jewish Center, I went
to the dedication of the Hebrew University on Mount Scopus.
We were there again in 1934, when, as the National Chairman
of the United Synagogue Campaign to build a Synagogue
Center in Jerusalem, I was privileged to lay the cornerstone
of what is now the Yeshurun Synagogue on King George
Boulevard. And now we have returned from our third visit of
ten glorious weeks.

1) Psalms, 122:6.

When I compare what I saw on these three trips, I recall an interesting comment of our Rabbis. They ask, "Why was the Temple in Jerusalem known as the House of Jacob?" It would have been more logical for it to be known as the House of Abraham, the founder of our faith and father of our people, or the House of Isaac, who was ready to sacrifice his life for his faith. "All three", they tell us, "stood on the site on which the future Temple was to be built. Abraham saw it as a mountain, 'the mountain of Moriah'; Isaac saw it as a field, 'he went out to pray in the field'; Jacob saw it in his vision as a house, 'this is none other but a House of God'; and because he saw it as a completed house, the Temple bore his name, *Bet Yaakov*, House of Jacob."[2]

In 1925, I saw Palestine as a mountain; wherever I turned I saw mountains of difficulties which appeared insurmountable. Little did anyone dream at that time that within less than a generation these gigantic obstacles would be removed. In 1934, I saw Palestine as a field: flourishing settlements with cultivated land and thriving orange groves on sites that used to be filled with mountain rocks. We saw a new Jerusalem that was beginning to develop beyond the old city and a new Tel-Aviv that was beginning to look like a town with a future. But in our most recent visit, we saw Palestine transformed into Israel, the House, the *bayit*, the home, in the literal sense of the term, of the children of Jacob. That is what Israel is today, the home of the Jew, of every Jew who wants to return to his ancestral-new home. I saw there a land with two million inhabitants, where Jews from all parts of the world find an open door, a warm welcome to greet them, where they feel at home.

In Israel to-day one beholds a new Jew, a transformed Jew. I am reminded of a beautiful folk tale which our Rabbis relate, that "when the Messiah will come, all the dead Jews, buried in the various lands of their dispersion, will roll from their

2) Pesachim, 88a; Rashi to Genesis, 28:17.

graves until their bodies will touch the soil of Israel, and then the Holy One, blessed be He, will bestow within them the spirit of life and they will stand erect."[3]

This Messianic miracle we are beginning to behold in Israel. Jews, who were literally dead in the far flung hells of Europe, Asia, and Africa, have after many hardships, as if rolling underground, finally touched the soil of Israel, and, lo and behold, they are suddenly infused with the breath of a new life and now stand erect. That is the great achievement of Israel: the fashioning of a new Jew, no longer the Jew with the bent back, cringing before his enemies. You see there the fulfillment of God's promise, "And I shall lead you *kommemiyut*, standing erect,"[4] *b'komah zekufah*, "in full stature and unafraid before any human being," as the Rabbis significantly interpret the Biblical words.[5]

I visited a *kibbutz*, a settlement of young people, which was close to the Gaza border. I watched them as they went about their work, tilling the soil and tending to their flocks. Each goes about his work as did his ancestors after their first return from exile, "with one hand wrought in the work, and the other holding his weapon."[6] Wholly unafraid, they go prepared with their guns should they be needed to repulse an enemy attack.

And one sees there a happy people. Hitler, in one of his last speeches, boasted: "We will see to it that never will the Jew laugh any more." How false was his prediction! In Israel the Jew laughs and sings. The vision of the Psalmist is fulfilled: "When the Lord will return the captivity of Zion..... then our mouth shall be filled with laughter, and our tongue with song."[7] One sees the happy dancing in the streets of the cities and villages, the laughter and the singing of old and young even in the settlements close to the enemies' lands.

3) Genesis Rabbah, 96:7.
4) Leviticus, 26:13.
5) Genesis Rabbah, 12:5.
6) Nehemiah, 4:11.
7) Psalms, 126:1-2.

You see in Israel not only a reborn Jew but also a reborn soil. It is remarkable to note that for 1900 years the land had been settled by other peoples, Romans, Christians of every land, Turks and Arabs, all of whom had tried to work the soil; but the soil refused to respond. The hills and valleys remained studded with massive rocks, and no one could make the soil fertile, it stubbornly remained desolate. It was, as the Bible described it, "a land which devours its inhabitants."[8] But as the Rabbis interpreted these words: "They (the Jews) thought that these words bespoke bad tidings; but they were meant for their good. For all other peoples it will be a land which devours its inhabitants, but not for the Jew!"[9]

And the truth of these words is so evident today. The land that had been without its people now willingly responds to the people that had been without its land. It is as if the soil, too, now laughs and is happy to yield its flowers, its fruits, its vegetation to the efforts of the people for whom she has waited nineteen centuries. True, the change did not come easily; it was "a land whose stones were iron."[10] But again, as the Rabbis interpreted this phrase, "Do not read *avoneha*, its stones, but *boneha*, its builders."[11] The builders in Israel were and are of iron spirit, with iron determination. With their bare hands they removed the rocks from the hills and tilled the barren soil.

Israel is a land of meager natural resources, but it is abundantly blessed with human resources. In this rebirth of the soil of Israel, the Jewish National Fund has played a remarkable role. The trees, the forests, and the soil reclamation that you behold wherever you turn are the clearest evidence of the great contribution this organization has made in this historic transformation.

You see too, in Israel, the miracle of a language reborn. He-

8) Numbers, 13:32.
9) Sotah, 35a.
10) Deuteronomy, 8:9.
11) Taanit, 4a.

brew was never dead; but for 1900 years it has been the language of the scholar, the sage, the writer. In Israel today it is
the language of the street and market place, of the schools
and university, of physician and attorney, of merchant and
scientist. And the old Jewish culture and the hunger for Jewish knowledge have again come to life. The Jews of Israel are
once more the People of the Book. Despite the meager in-
come of the average Jew in Israel, more books are published,
sold and read there, proportionate to the population, than in
any other land.

What impresses a tourist greatly, is the tremendous pace of
development in every part of the land and in every sphere of
activity. The Israelis seem to be racing against time; they are
eager to make up for their loss during the centuries they were
separated from their land. You see this progress not only in
the erection of homes and factories, but in the magnificent
structures which house the social, the philanthropic, the cultural, and the educational institutions. One must feel over-
whelmed gazing at the impressive Hadassah hospital and medical school, at the magnificent buildings of the Hebrew University, at the imposing structures of the Weizmann Institute
and the Technion, at the artistic beauty of the Mann Auditorium and the Rubin Academy of Music, and even at the
more modest Bar Ilan University, and the hospitals and charitable institutions throughout the land.

And also in the field of religion you see a remarkable growth
and development: the new and modern structures of some of
the old and newer *Yeshivot* — schools for the study of the ancient, classic, religious texts; the academies of research that
have sprung into being in the last decade or two; the new buildings which are being erected by the Jewish Theological Seminary and the Hebrew Union College to serve their students in
Israel. In this sphere, one stands in awe before the newly erected *Hekal Shlomo* in Jerusalem, which is the official seat of
the Chief Rabbinate, and includes a beautiful synagogue.

What dignity this masterpiece of architecture adds to the traditional faith of our people, which had usually been associated only with the old, deteriorated synagogues in the Old City.

Religion in Israel is also involved in rebirth. A host of novel problems, arising from everyday life, now confront the Rabbinate. No longer dealing solely with abstract questions or with ancient practices alone, the religious authorities are endeavoring to meet the challenges posed by modern needs and interests.

The miracle we behold in reborn Israel today is due above all to the spirit of self-sacrifice that marks the lives of young and old in every part of the land. They have the faith that God's promise will be fulfilled, and they reinforce that faith with the determination to do everything to make the promise a reality. You see that sacrificial spirit in their everyday lives, in their willingness to share their homes and their substance with the new immigrants until new homes are available. And you note it particularly in their heroic acceptance of the loss of sons and husbands and other loved ones who made the supreme sacrifice in the War of Independence and in the other battles that had been forced upon them. There is hardly a home which has not sustained such loss. The populace accepts this sacrifice with dignity and gratitude and with what could aptly be called pride that such sacrifice brought hope and salvation to the people whom the fallen ones loved, as Rabbi Akiba did, not only with mind and heart but with all their soul. What a challenge such sacrifice is to American Jews, many of whom think that they make a sacrifice when they respond with a contribution to the United Jewish Appeal!

It is related of the prophet Jeremiah that "when he returned to Jerusalem from Babylon, he found the fingers of the dead hands of the fallen warriors, fighting in defense of Judea, scattered among the hills. Lovingly he gathered them, embraced and kissed them, and wrapped them in his *talit*, his garment or prayer shawl.'"[12] Here we have in poetic form the message that American Jewry should take to heart. We, too, symbolically speaking, should take the memory of the bones of those gallant martyrs, lovingly embrace them, and wrap them in our *talit* when we stand in prayer before our Father in Heaven. That memory will inspire us to do our share, in fullest measure, in this historic drama of our people's regeneration.

I do not wish to imply, even for a moment, that the act of rebirth is now complete, that all is now well, and that the people are now at ease in Zion. Many are the problems that face Israel; but the problems are altogether different from those which our people had to face through the centuries of exile. These are problems dealing with life not with death, with the growth of a living organism not with a stifled existence.

The Rabbis, in our classic literature, relate a quaint anecdote: "The daughter of Rabbi Gamaliel gave birth to a child. When the sage visited her, she said to him: 'Father, give me your blessing.' And he replied, 'May the word *woe* never depart from your lips.' 'Father!' she cried in fright. 'I asked for a blessing but that was a curse!' 'No, my child,' he replied, 'it is a blessing. As long as a child lives, a parent always finds something to complain about: Woe is me that my child does not eat enough; woe is me that my child does not study enough; there is always cause for woe with a child that is alive.'"[13] Yea, many are the times when our people in Israel cry *woe* in their efforts to solve the problems that face them. But these *woes* are different woes from those our fathers uttered in their exile. These are woes that come from life and from the throes of growth of a living people.

The greatest problem that faces our brethren in Israel and us is, of course, the enmity of the Arab nations which surround them; not the enmity, I am convinced, of the Arab peoples,

12) Pesichta, Lamentations Rabbah, 34.
13) Genesis Rabbah, 26:7.

but of their leaders who, in order to keep the masses blinded to the economic and social misery in which they find themselves and to the condition of illiteracy and ignorance in which they are kept, use the existence of Israel as a convenient scapegoat for their nefarious purpose. But the hatred is there, and Israel is aware of it, though unafraid.

There is but one answer to that hatred, and that answer must be given not only by our brethren in Israel but also by us Jews of America. And the answer is given to us in the Bible. There we read how the patriarch Isaac returns to the place where his father Abraham had dug wells to nourish his life. Isaac comes to restore these wells of living waters and begins to prosper in his endeavors. But the Philistines come to him and cry: "Go from us for thou hast become too prosperous for us." And they destroyed the wells he dug, and fought with him. Did Isaac give up his efforts and yield to this destructive opposition? Oh no; "He called this place *esek*, strife, for they fought with him;" and he dug new wells. Again they filled the wells with dirt, and they hated him. Did Isaac yield to that hatred? Again, no! "He called the site *sitnah*, hatred" and continued to dig and to dig new wells, until they no longer strove over it, and he called the place *Rechovot*, "for now the Lord hath made room for us, and we shall be fruitful in the land!"[14] How modern this tale sounds; how history has repeated itself! The people of Israel have gone through these various stages. They returned to the land where their fathers had lived and started to dig and to restore the wells of life which their fathers had once dug but which now were dried and lay waste. And when they began to prosper they, too, were told: "Go from us, for you have become too prosperous for us," and their wells were destroyed. They went through the stage of *esek*, of strife; continuous attacks of marauders, a war waged against them by five Arab nations. But they kept digging their wells. And now,

14) Genesis, 26:13-22.

there is the stage of *sitnah*, of hatred, fostered and enflamed by the false leaders of these Arab masses. Our answer to this present hatred must be the answer given by Isaac. They in Israel and we in America must continue to dig and to dig wells, springs of life, not to falter for a moment, until the day comes, as it came for Isaac, when again it will be said: "And they strove no more," and all the land will be known as *Rechovot*, "for now the Lord hath made room for us and we shall be fruitful in the land!"

The Religion of Israel
and the Land of Israel

Address delivered at Brooklyn Academy of Music, May 31, 1943, on the occasion of the presentation of the Rabbi Israel H. Levinthal Forest in Israel by Brooklyn Jewry. The introductory statements are omitted.

Since you have deemed it fitting to honor me, I would like to express my gratitude for your thoughtfulness in presenting me with this particular type of gift, one which will link my name with the new life in the old-new land of our people, Eretz Israel. It is quite appropriate, in paying tribute to a Rabbi, a teacher of the Jewish religion, to associate his name with Eretz Israel.

There is a striking passage in the pages of our Talmud that I wish to quote to you. A Rabbi says: *Il'ma'le chatu Yisrael, lo nitnu lahem ela chamishah chumshe Torah v'sefer Yeho-shua bilvad.* "Had not Israel sinned, God would have given to them not the twenty-four books that make up our Bible, but only six books, the five books of Moses and the *sefer Yeho-shua*, the Book of Joshua alone."[2] Mind you, this Rabbi links the five books of Moses only with the Book of Joshua. Of all the books in the Bible, this one book is chosen to stand on equal footing with the Pentateuch, the five books of Moses; and he gives us this reason: *mipne sh'erkah shel eretz Yisrael hu*, "The Book of Joshua describes the land of Palestine." It gives us the dimensions, the measurements of Palestine; it emphasizes the importance of Palestine. This Rabbi could not

1) Nedarim, 22b.

conceive of the Pentateuch without the *sefer Yehoshua.* One without the other is like a body without a soul, or like a soul without a body.

We have just heard, in the eloquent words of Dr. Stephen S. Wise, of a distinction which opponents of Zionism have made between the Jewish religion and the rebirth of Eretz Israel, as if there were a conflict between the two. How little those critics understand what this great sage of the Talmud had in mind. You cannot speak of the Jewish religion without the *sefer Yehoshua.* You cannot separate the two. The ancient Jews in Greece, historians tell us, spoke not of the *Pentateuch,* not of the *five* books of Moses, but of the *Hexateuch,* the six books. The book of Joshua was linked with the *chamishah chumshe Torah.* And if you want to know what Zionism really is, what its underlying philosophy is, I say it is to bring back the natural link between the *chamishah chumshe Torah* and the *sefer Yehoshua.* There is no question of priority here, whether it is religion or Eretz Israel that comes first; together they form a unity in the fundamental needs of the Jew.

Again I must turn to the teachings of our ancient sages. The Midrash records a unique discussion between the two great schools of thought in Jewish life, the *Bet Hillel* and the *Bet Shammai,* the School of Hillel and the School of Shammai. The discussion deals with a strange subject: "Which was created first, the heavens or the earth?"

The *Bet Shammai* said, *hashamayim niv'reu techilah,* "The heavens were created first." The *Bet Hillel* said, *haaretz nivrat techilah,* "The earth was created first." Each school was able to quote verses from the Bible to support its premise. One Rabbi, however, who sat and listened to this discussion, Rabbi Simeon ben Yochoi, a great teacher, philosopher, and mystic, said, *tamihah ani,* "I am surprised," *he'ek nechleku avot haolam,* "how these great men argue about such a matter! It is all so very simple, *shenehem nivreu yachdav,* they were both created at one time!"[2] And he, too, quoted a verse from the Bible to prove his words: *koray ani alehem yaamdu yachdav.* God said, "when I call unto them they stand up together."[3] There is no conflict between heaven and earth, between the spiritual values of religion and those of the land of Israel, both were fashioned simultaneously in the mind and soul of the Jew! That is the underlying philosophy of Zionism.

Our tragedy for the last 1,900 years was simply this: we lived in the *shamayim*, in the *heavens* alone. We had no foothold anywhere on God's earth. "*Luft menschen*," the great Max Nordau called us. Zionism says: we want to retain the *shamayim*, we want the Jewish religion, we want to further the old Jewish prophetic ideals; but we need also *eretz*, we need the land, the land that gave birth to that religion, the land that saw the flowering of that religion, the land that has so much yet to contribute to the religious life of the entire world.

And the Jewish National Fund, about which you have heard so much tonight, also has this further end. It wishes to link the *shamayim* with the *eretz*. That is the philosophy of the Jewish National Fund: land which God had created to be a blessing, but which through personal speculation and desire for aggrandizement has become a curse and a cause of so much misery in so many places must again become a source of blessedness. The land of the Jewish National Fund can never provoke that curse because that land can never be owned by any individual, can never be sold or irrevocably parted with. It belongs throughout eternity to all the people of Israel.

All our work in Eretz Israel has this one aim: to bring the *shamayim* closer to the *eretz*. What did we Jews first do when we came to that land? Did we start with the building of factories? Did we start with the creating of trusts? We built a University! We wanted the *shamayim* to fuse with the *eretz*. We

2) Genesis Rabbah, 1:21.
3) Isaiah, 48:13.

built synagogues; we built academies of learning, all because
we wanted the *shamayim* to be joined with the *eretz*. We wanted the *eretz* upon which the *shamayim* could become a bene-
ficent and inspiring influence.

Now, because Zionism has this consecrated objective, which
is so harmonious with the Four Freedoms, we felt justified
in believing that the nations of the world would help us realize
our aspiration. But, alas, the Jew appears to be the forgotten
man of the world. It seems as if the great powers think of the
future of all peoples except the Jewish people.

Nevertheless, our gathering here tonight is an expression of
our faith in the conscience of Christendom and in the conscience of the democratic powers. We will not lose our faith.
We refuse to believe that the Bermuda conference[4] has uttered
the last word in answer to our aims. We have faith in the words,
the beautiful words in support of our goal that had previously
come from the great leaders of our own country, of Great Britain, of all our allied powers; and, because we have faith, we
go on buying land and planting trees in Palestine, we continue
to send Jews into Palestine because we know that eventually
the historic justice, due the Jewish people, will be realized.

Last week, we read in the synagogue for our Haftorah, the
Scriptural lesson, a dramatic tale. Little Palestine was being
besieged by the Babylonian army. Jeremiah, the great prophet, was in a dungeon. He saw his land becoming desolate, his
beloved people being slaughtered in the streets of Jerusalem.
But just then, he heard God's voice speaking to him, *K'ne
leka hasadeh bakesef*, "buy thee the land for money," *ki leka
mishpat hageulah liknot*, "for you have the right of redemp-

4) The Bermuda Conference held in April 1943, called by the United
States and Great Britain to devise measures for the rescue of Jewish refugees from Germany and other Nazi dominated lands, which
terminated with no solution offered, and at which the memoran-
dum presented by representatives of American Jewry which called
upon England to open the doors of Palestine remained unheeded.

tion to purchase it."[5] And he did. Precisely when all others were surrendering hope, thinking that it was the end of Palestine for all time, he bought his inheritance in Eretz Israel, saw to it that the deed was sealed, and put it away in a safe place. It was the evidence of his faith that God's promise would yet be fulfilled: "houses and fields and vineyards shall yet again be bought in this land."[6]

And tonight, too, in these days when things look dark before our eyes, when we hear that the White Paper has not yet been repealed, we hear the command of God, *k'ne leka hasadeh*, buy the field and buy the land in Eretz Israel, *ki leka mishpat hageula liknot*, for you have the right of redemption, the moral right, the historic right, the legal right to redeem that land!

We know our task is not easy; we know that many obstacles and many hardships are in our path. But again I say, this gathering tonight is evidence of what is felt in the hearts of all the Jews throughout the world, that we refuse to go backward, and are determined to go forward.

Only a few weeks ago we celebrated the festival of Passover. We recounted how the Jews had left the land of Egypt. You remember that story, of how suddenly they turned around and saw Pharaoh and his army marching toward them to bring them back to bondage in Egypt. They wanted to go farther but could not. The waters of the Red Sea lay before them. "What shall we do? What shall we do?" they cried. At that moment God's voice was heard: "Speak to the children of Israel, let them go forward."[7] But how could they go forward facing, as they were, the waters of the Red Sea? The Bible tells us that a miracle occurred, the waters divided and the Israelites passed on dry land. That is all the Bible says.

The Rabbis in the Midrash, however, tell us more. They

5) Jeremiah, 32:7, 25.
6) *Ibid.*, v. 15.
7) Exodus, 14:15.

tell us how that miracle took place. Miracles do not happen just by themselves. Do you know when the waters divided? *Lo nikra lahem ha-yam*, "the waters refused to be divided, *ad sh'bau l'toko ad chotman*, until the Jews first plunged into the waters ready to drown and to sacrifice themselves for their ideal. Only when the waters were *ad chotman*, up to their very nostrils, and the Jews were almost drowning, then did the waters divide, and the miracle occur!"[8] That is how miracles happen: when people are ready to make sacrifices for their ideal, when they go forward despite obstacles and difficulties. And I take this meeting as an evidence of our determination to keep going forward, forward, and forward in our work until success is finally achieved.

And one word more. This is a twofold Decoration Day. It is a Memorial Day for the American heroes who have died, and it is also one on which the Jews memorialize their dead heroes. As a matter of fact, we Jews are in the midst of a period of mourning, not only the mourning of the *sefirah*[9] for a tragedy that occurred centuries ago, but also a period of mourning proclaimed by the Synagogue Council of America. In these weeks we are to give expression to our sense of sorrow for the death of the millions of "*kedoshim*," Jewish martyrs who perished in Nazi-controlled lands in Europe. Many of you must know the old Jewish custom of placing a little bit of earth from Eretz Israel upon the eyes of a deceased person. Many a poor Jew would work and toil and starve in order to save enough money to purchase this precious earth from Palestine. He treasured this earth, so that it might be placed upon his eyes when he died. And the belief became current that once

8) Exodus Rabbah, 21:9.
9) The period of mourning observed between the conclusion of Passover and the beginning of the month of Sivan, commemorating, according to Jewish tradition, the tragic death of the thousands of pupils of Rabbi Akiba. *Cf.* Yebamot, 62b; Shulchan Aruk, Orach Chayim, 493:1, 2.

this precious soil were placed upon the eyes of the dead, when *techiyat ha-metim*, when the resurrection came, that body would find itself revived in Eretz Israel.

Millions of martyrs to German brutality died without the blessed privilege of having the soil of Palestine on their eyes. Let us dedicate ourselves to perform for them this *mitzvah*, this sacred obligation. We cannot actually put this earth upon their eyes, but let us determine that for each one of those martyrs a separate tree will be planted on the soil that they loved, and that another tree, another garden, another grove, another *dunam* of earth, will be redeemed. Then we too shall witness a *techiyat ha-metim*, a new resurrection, the resurrection of the *Am Yisrael*, the people of Israel — a new, living people of Israel — on that old-new land of Israel, *Eretz Yisrael!*

A Book of
Only Two Sentences

Address delivered at Commencement Exercises of the Jewish Theological Seminary of America, June 8, 1958, dedicated to the Tenth Anniversary of the establishment of the State of Israel.

I am ever conscious of the Talmudic injunction: *L'olam tehe emat tzibur aleka*, "One must always have great respect for the congregation or the audience before whom he stands."[1] The phrase *emat tzibur* connotes something more than *respect*. It really means *fear, trepidation*. I have that *emat tzibur* every time I address my congregation. You can imagine, dear friends, what a double portion of *emat tzibur* I have today when I address you in the presence of my teachers and my masters, the intellectual giants among our people today.

It is most fitting that these commencement exercises be dedicated to the theme of Zion reborn. This institution, our beloved Seminary, from its very inception has been closely aligned with the Zionist ideal. The students, the graduates, and many of the faculty have been actively identified with the Zionist movement. We are proud of the fact that two of our distinguished alumni served as national presidents of the Zionist Organization of America.[2] We recall the tremendous impact made upon American Jewry half-a-century ago by the historic statement of the late Professor Solomon Schechter, emphasizing the spiritual aspects of the movement, a statement which won thousands of new adherents to the Zionist cause.

The United Synagogue of America and the Women's

1) Sotah, 40a.
2) Dr. Israel Goldstein and the late Dr. Solomon Goldman.

League have also created a link with the land of Israel. On King George Boulevard, in the city of Jerusalem, stands a magnificent building now serving as a model synagogue of the Jeshurun congregation, which was the gift of these two organizations to the people of Jerusalem. I am privileged to recall that I, myself, served as the national chairman of the campaign for that gift; and the honor had been given to me in the year 1934 to lay the cornerstone of that historic synagogue. And now the Seminary is engaged in a new venture, a further link between this institution and the Land of Israel, a project to erect a dormitory and a Center in the city of Jerusalem for our students who will pursue part of their academic studies in the *avirah d'Eretz Yisrael,* in the atmosphere of the Land of Israel. And so you can see, dear friends, that we are *mechutanim* in this *simchah,* that we have a right as close relatives to participate in this joyous celebration.

In order to properly evaluate the significance of the historic miracle which occurred just ten years ago, the establishment of the State of Israel, I would like you to recall with me a passage in the Torah lesson which we read in the synagogue just yesterday morning. The Bible describes the journeying of the Israelites in the wilderness on their way from Egypt to the promised land. In the midst of this description, the Bible pauses to tell us: "And it came to pass, when the Ark journeyed that Moses said: 'Arise, O Lord, and let Thine enemies be scattered; and let them that hate Thee be dispersed before Thee.' And when it rested, he said: 'Return, O Lord, unto the tens of thousands of the families of Israel.' "[3] These two verses are familiar to all of you, even to those of you not fully acquainted with your Bible, because they form part of our liturgy. We recite the first verse every Sabbath, every festive day, when we take the Torah from the Ark. And we recite the second verse when we return the Torah to the Ark.

3) Numbers, 10:35, 36.

Now, those of you who read the Hebrew text must have noticed, I am sure, something strange as you looked at these words. There is a special marking at the beginning and at the end of these verses — somewhat like brackets — which you do not find anywhere else in the entire five books of Moses. In this unique marking the letter *nun* is turned backwards both before and at the end of these two verses. We call it in Hebrew the *nun hafukah*, "the *nun* that is turned backward." Something very significant must be told by these verses, otherwise, why should they have these special signs?

One Rabbi in the Talmud tells us that "God Himself placed these markings at the beginning and at the end of this passage."[4] Another Rabbi, adding to this comment, says that "these two verses form a *sefer chashuv b'atzmo*, an important book in themselves."[5] Mind you, a book, an entire book, of just two sentences! And a *sefer chashuv*, a very important book! This Rabbi goes further, declaring that we make a mistake in thinking that there are only five books of Moses. "There are *shivah sifre Torah*, seven books of the Torah."[6] Beside Genesis, Exodus, Leviticus and Deuteronomy, he divides Numbers into three books — one book before these verses, one book after them, and one consisting only of two verses, making seven books in all. And a modern commentator emphasizes this theory by stating "that because of the great importance of the content of these two verses, it is fitting that we regard these two verses as a book in themselves."[7]

I should like to analyze for you this book of just two verses. I see in this little book not merely a record or description of something that happened three thousand years ago when the Israelites were in the wilderness of Sinai; but also a prophetic summary of the challenges that faced the Jews in the nineteen

4) Shabbat, 115b, 116a.
5) *Ibid.*
6) *Ibid.*
7 Torah Temimah, to Numbers, 10:35.

hundred years since being driven from their land. In the phrase, "*When the Ark journeyed*," the Ark is a synonym for the Jew. It was not only that the Jew carried the Ark, but that *haaron nosey et nosav*, "the Ark carried the Jew."[8] It is as if the text had said, "*When the Jew journeyed*." What was the one problem that always faced him, the one plea that came from his lips, in these nineteen hundred years of his journeying? "Arise, O Lord, and may Thine enemies be scattered!" The Bible uses the words: "Thine enemies," and "they that hate Thee, O God;" and the Rabbis are quick to tell us that "these are really the haters of the Jew."[9] They hate the Jew because they hate the God of the Jew. They cannot forgive the Jew for having brought the Torah from Heaven, the Torah of truth, justice, mercy, and love. Psychologists, economists, sociologists, all advance different reasons for the rise and existence of anti-Semitism. There is, of course, some truth in each of their theories, but the Rabbis go to the root of anti-Semitism when they give the definition of the word Sinai, the mountain on which the Torah was revealed: *sh'misham yardah sinah l'umot haolam alav*, "It was on the mountain of *Sinai* that *sinah*, hatred, descended to the hearts of many people toward the Jew."[10] That is how we have to understand that passage in the Talmud.

This then, was the problem that faced the Jew in every land and in every age: how to withstand the hatred of the world, how to disperse the enemies of God and of himself. Everywhere and at all times the prayer came from the lips of the Jew, "May Thine enemies be scattered before Thee!" How much energy did we Jews have to exert; how many millions of dollars have we had to spend fighting this disease of anti-Semitism, even here in America. Thank God, we have rid America

8) *Cf.* Exodus Rabbah, 36:4; Numbers Rabbah, 4:21.
9) Rashi to verse 35.
10) Shabbat, 89a.

of this malady in large measure; but we still need our defense organizations, and American Jewry is still asked to give of its funds for that purpose.

We come now to the second chapter constituted by the second verse of this miniature book. And that chapter begins ten years ago with the miracle of Israel reborn. *"And when the Ark rested,"* when the Jew at last found a home in which to rest his weary bones, there was an immediate transformation in him and in his problem. Thanks to God, we have witnessed and are witnessing the realization of that prayer of Moses: "Return, O Lord, unto the tens of thousands of the families of Israel!" Tens of thousands of our people have returned to this new home of Israel and not only has there been a change in the problem and the concern of the Jew, but also in the Jew himself.

It is true that we have enemies today, too. Israel itself is surrounded by enemies. But it is a different kind of enemy that the Jew now faces, a political enemy. For the problem this creates we hope there will be a speedy solution. But the Jew faced by this different enemy is himself a different Jew. No longer is he Jacob cringing at the heel of Esau; he is *Yisrael*, a prince of God, who stands erect, with straightened back, *v'lo yereim mishum briah*, "unafraid of anyone."[11] That is the miracle which has occurred in these last ten years. And we Jews in America can be proud that we played an important role in the realization of that prayer of Moses: "Return, O Lord, unto the tens of thousands of the families of Israel!" Because of our sacrifices tens of thousands of Jews have found a new home. But we shall have to do much more. The work is not yet finished; the way is still long; and we must dedicate ourselves to the complete and continued fulfillment of that prayer.

But that miracle of the past decade has had its effect not only on the Jew in Israel but also on the Jew in America. Com-

11) Genesis Rabbah, 12:5.

menting on God's promise: *v'olek etkem kommemiyut*, "And I shall lead you standing erect,"[12] the Rabbis noticed that the word *kommemiyut* is not in the singular but in the dual form. The text speaks of *shtey komot*, "two standing erect."[13] Yea, this comment may be applied to the miracle of our day. The Jew in Israel now stands erect, and we Jews in the diaspora, particularly in America, stand erect too, in new stature, in new self-respect, and in new self-esteem. The miracle has transformed us as well. We had Jewish *metim* here, dead Jews. Their bodies seemed to function, *guf kayam*, "the body was preserved but it was a *serefat neshamah*, their souls, their Jewish souls, were consumed."[14] Tens of thousands of American Jews had wandered away from all Jewish interests, had divorced themselves from the peoplehood of Israel. But now, with the miracle of the touch of the soil of Israel, they too have been transformed; and they too have taken on *ruach chayim*, a spirit of life.

We speak of the religious revival that is taking place in American Jewish life. It is true there is a revival. Membership in all synagogues is increasing by the day; more children flock to the Hebrew Schools. We dare not minimize this revival. At least the people want to be Jews. There is a searching. But it is only in its beginning.

Maurice Samuel, the brilliant writer and lecturer, who perhaps more than anyone else has the pulse of American Jewry because of his contact with so many audiences, made a fine observation just about a year or two ago. He said that, in former years, when he lectured to Jewish audiences, the first question, without exception, that was always put to him during the question period was: "*Why* should I be a Jew?" Today, he says, he never hears that question. Another question is now asked: "*How* can I be a Jew?" As he says: "These young parents,

12) Leviticus, 26:13.
13) Genesis Rabbah, *ibid.*, Tanchuma, Genesis, 6.
14) Sanhedrin, 52a.

whom I now see by the thousands in my audiences, were never drawn to Judaism by argument. Only reality touched them. The most effective influence in this transformation was the creation of the State of Israel." Above all, he notes, "there is a readiness to listen, an openness to the new that makes this generation, to use Ludwig Lewisohn's phrase, 'so accessible to God.' "

In fact, we have evidence of a resurgence of religious interest among the youth of all denominations in America, particularly among the college youth. R. Richard Niebuhr, commenting on this change in the atmosphere of the college campus, tells us: "Youth is seeking — fumbling often — to reclaim the ancestral ground on which previous generations were nurtured, but which they abandoned."[15] The Jewish college student is no exception. Will Herberg, a keen observer of college youth, tells us: "I can say without qualification that interest in, and concern with religion, as manifested by the present student generation — Jewish and non-Jewish alike — is something really extraordinary and is constantly growing. I have no hesitation in confirming the testimony of Professor Stuart Hughes of Harvard, who states with some surprise: 'The avant-garde of students is becoming old-fashioned. Religion is now the latest thing.' "[16]

Here is the challenge to you, young men, who have been ordained today in the Rabbinate — and the challenge to you, young men and women, who have graduated as teachers — and even the challenge to you, the new cantors of the synagogues. It is for you to satisfy that yearning, to give our people the spiritual and cultural nourishment that will fulfill their desire to be Jews.

There is one further concluding thought that I wish to bring

15) Quoted by Will Herberg, "Religious Trends in American Jewry," *Judaism*, (July, 1954), p. 236.
16) *Ibid.*, p. 234; *Cf.* Stuart Hughes, in *Saturday Review*, (March 3, 1951).

to you. What we want in *Eretz Yisrael* is something more than just a resting place for the weary body of the Jew. We want something for the *neshamah* of the Jew, for his soul. Just as we desire a return of the body, so we desire a return of the genius — the spiritual and cultural genius — of the Jew. Were I to express what our hearts feel as to what we expect of Israel, I would put it in one verse of the Bible — the first Biblical verse in which the Jew is linked with *Eretz Yisrael* — the words that God spoke to Abraham: *lek leka*, "go thee from thy land. . . . to the land which *areka*, I will show thee."[17] That is how we usually translate the verse. But it seems to me that this translation is not altogether correct.

I have a very simple question to pose. Just a few verses before the last verses in *Noah*, we read that "Terach took Abraham his son and Sarah, the wife of Abraham. . . . and they went forth. . . . to go into the land of Canaan."[18] They only stopped for a brief while at Charan. Abraham knew where he was going; he knew that he was going to Canaan. Why, then, should the text say: "to the land which I will show thee"? I believe that there is an altogether different meaning in these words. I realize that I am speaking before great Hebraists and it is therefore with some trepidation that I offer my own interpretation, but I think it is a correct one. The word *areka* in Hebrew has two meanings: it can mean "which I will show thee," referring to the land, the land which I will show you; and it can also mean "where I will show *you*," you, Abraham.

The commentator Rashi catches this deeper meaning of the word. He tells us that God said to Abraham: "Go thee to the land, *asher areh tivaka l'olam*, where I will show your nature, your true self to the world."[19] Abraham's going to Canaan was to reveal to the Jew and to the world his true self, his true genius. And that is why God says to him *lek leka*, *go thee*, a most

17) Genesis, 12:1.
18) *Ibid.*, 11:31.
19) Rashi, to Genesis, 12:1.

unusual phrase. The Hebrew word for "go" is *lek*, that is the common expression for "to go." *Lek leka* is found only twice in the entire Bible. But the phrase means something more than merely "to go." It means, literally, *"go to thy self!"* What God wanted Abraham to do was to go back to himself, to his own soul, to his own genius.

And that is what we expect and hope of the Jew who has returned to Israel. We want the Jew in Israel to show his true soul to the world. We want the Jew in Israel to go back to his spiritual self, to his own Bible, to his own prophets, to his own sages, to his own philosophers and poets, in short, to be himself!

And that is what we would like to see also in America through the influence of *Eretz Yisrael*. Thank God we are already witnessing in Israel a resurgence of the Jewish spirit. We are impatient. We would like to see it proceed more rapidly. And we want American Jewry to be influenced by the flowering of that Jewish culture. There is to be in Israel a fountain source to give Jews in America guidance and inspiration. As was said of the holy Temple in Jerusalem, so we hope it may be said of Israel: *she'misham shaavu ruach hakodesh*, "that from there they drew the inspiration of the Holy Spirit."[20] We wish to become influenced, so that the American Jew too can go back to himself, his real self, and thus make known to the world the real nature of the Jew.

It is to that task, my dear young friends, that we urge you to dedicate yourselves today. And as you go out to the length and breadth of this land, to your own communities, to be with them and to serve them, we offer a fervent prayer to our Father in Heaven: *Yiten Hashem cheno alekem b'kal makom she'atem holkim*, "May the Grace of God accompany you in all your paths in life!"[21]

20) Genesis Rabbah, 70:8.
21) Cf. Numbers Rabbah, 11:13.

Ben Gurion's Plea
to American Jewry

Preached on first day of Passover,
April 1, 1961.

I should like to pose at this time what I think is an interesting question. It deals with the early Israelites in the land of Egypt. All of you, of course, know that on this festival of Passover we celebrate the redemption of our people from their Egyptian bondage. They had been enslaved there for 210 years. According to an ancient tradition, they had been in Egypt for 400 years, in other words, 180 years before they actually became slaves.

I think you know the story of how and why they originally came to the land of Egypt. The patriarch Jacob and his family had first lived in Canaan. You recall that Joseph had been sold by his brothers as a slave and was taken to Egypt. Later he was imprisoned and while in prison he correctly interpreted the dreams of Pharaoh's two servants. We are then told that Pharaoh dreamt dreams which no one could interpret, and Joseph was released from the prison in order to do so. His interpretation satisfied Pharaoh. The dreams, he said, foretold the coming of seven years of plenty to be followed by seven years of famine. And that is exactly what happened.

Now, during the seven lean years the famine not only affected Egypt, but the neighboring land of Canaan as well, and Jacob and his children suffered a lack of food. Jacob, thereupon, told his sons to go down to Egypt to purchase food. And you know what happened. Joseph, now an important fig-

159

ure, recognized his brothers immediately, but they did not recognize him. At last, Joseph made himself known and asked that his father and the entire family be brought to the land of Egypt where provision had been made against famine. That was the beginning of the drama of the Jews in Egypt.

Now I have a simple question to ask. I do not know whether you have ever asked yourselves this question. Why did not these Israelites return to their land of Canaan at the end of the seven years of famine? After all, when the famine came to an end everyone had enough to eat. Why then did they remain in Egypt? Why did they not return to their own land? They had a home, the land of Canaan.

We can understand and excuse Jacob. After all, he had a son who was now the vice-ruler of Egypt and he wanted to enjoy that *nachat*, that pleasure, to bask in his reflected glory while being near his son. But then Jacob died. Before his death, he had shown his loyalty to his own land by making his children promise him that they would bury him immediately in Canaan. They fulfilled this promise. The whole family accompanied the coffin that bore Jacob's remains to Canaan, and they buried him there. But they returned to Egypt! Why did they not remain in their homeland rather than return to Egypt? Now that the famine was a thing of the past, and Joseph's father was dead they could have remained in Canaan.

Well, you might find an excuse for the brothers also. Inasmuch as their brother was a vice-ruler, they undoubtedly could enjoy special privileges as well as the pleasure of having one so close to them in such an exalted position. But then Joseph himself died. And while he had not asked to be immediately buried in Canaan, he had proven his loyalty to his own land in exacting a promise from his brothers that, when they returned to their land, they would take his body with them. Now that Joseph was dead, the brothers certainly had no apparent reason to remain. The question persists, why did they not go back to their own land? They could have avoided this entire chapter in Jewish history, the tragic 210 years of physical bondage.

Now you might argue: "It was so ordained by God. It was an historic necessity!" Had not God, in the days of the first patriarch, Abraham, said to him: "Know of a surety that thy seed shall be a stranger in a land that is not theirs, and shall serve them; and they shall afflict them four hundred years."[1]

But these words had not been spoken by God in terms of punishment; God simply had revealed to Abraham that which was going to be. God, according to Jewish teaching, is all-knowing. He knows what is going to happen; and He knew beforehand that the Israelites would remain in Egypt. But God gives man freedom of will, the ability to choose whatever path he desires. And the Israelites could freely have chosen to go back to their own land, the land of Canaan. The Rabbis explicitly tell us: "As long as even one of that group that originally came down to Egypt remained alive, there was no bondage, no compulsion whatever over the Israelites."[2] They could have done what they wanted. So the question remains: "Why did they stay in Egypt? Why did they not go back to their own land?"

I think the answer is a very simple one. The Israelites liked the life in Egypt. It was a much easier life than the one they had known in Canaan. There they had been shepherds and tillers of the soil. They had led a difficult, a primitive life. In Egypt there was industry, prosperity; and the Israelites enjoyed the pleasanter life there. They multiplied and they prospered. The Rabbis tell us, "They went to the Egyptian theatres and to their circuses,"[3] amusements they did not have in Canaan. Their love of the life in Egypt made them lose their desire to return to their own land.

Let us now pursue this chapter in history a little further. What happened when they remained in the land of Egypt?

1) Genesis, 15:13.
2) Exodus Rabbah, 1:7.
3) Yalkut Shimoni to Exodus, 1:7.

What was the consequence of their preference for this Egyptian life to the life in their own land? The consequences were two-fold. On the one hand, everything went along smoothly. They got along well with the Egyptians. There must have been national conferences between Egyptians and Israelites as well as brotherhood movements, just like our groups today. The Israelites got along so well, indeed, that the Rabbis tell us: "They started to assimilate with the Egyptians." They went so far that many of them even abolished the rite of circumcision; and they said: "Let us become like the Egyptians."[4] And the Egyptians encouraged them in the process of assimilation.

The Rabbis had a keen understanding of the deeper meaning of the Biblical text. We read in the Bible: "And they enslaved them *b'farek*, with hard labor."[5] The Rabbis read this verse differently; they make two words out of *b'farek — b'feh rak*, "they enslaved them with *smooth speech*."[6] The Egyptains said to the Israelites: "We are all brothers. Why should you be different from us? Why don't you accept our customs, our way of life?" And with that *peh rak*, with that smooth tongue of so-called brotherliness, of tolerance, they made the Israelites abandon their own traditions, their own way of life. Thus we see one consequence of their life in the new land, their gradual assimilation.

But there was another consequence. A new king came to power who did not know Joseph, who forgot what Joseph had done for the Egyptians. And then the real bondage began. The Egyptians really enslaved the Israelites *b'farek*, with hard labor. Now the Israelites wanted to return to their own land but they no longer could. The bars were down, and the new Pharaoh prohibited them from leaving the land. A similar situation exists today in Soviet Russia and in other Commu-

4) Exodus Rabbah, 1:10.
5) Exodus, 1:13.
6) Sotah, 11b; Exodus Rabbah, 1:15.

nist countries where the Jews would like to leave. If the doors were opened only slightly, hundreds of thousands of Jews would fly to Israel. But they cannot; it is too late.

These are the two consequences, the two possible consequences of the *galut*, of the dispersion. The smooth-speeched enslavement and the hard-labor enslavement. Both happened in Egypt. And we have to remember both these possibilities of *galut* life.

I have reviewed very briefly, of course, this chapter of the life of the Israelites in Egypt for a specific purpose. If you will read the Bible story in this new light, I think you will have a better appreciation of the famous and much publicized address which David Ben Gurion delivered a few months ago at the World Zionist Congress in Jerusalem. In urging world Jewry to migrate to Israel, the Prime Minister quoted the Talmudic passage: "Any Jew who lives outside of the land of Israel, is like one who has no God."[7] His speech aroused a great storm, not only of interest, but also of protest, of indignation, among many American Jews. Much has been written about it in the press, and much has been spoken about it from pulpit and platform throughout the land.

Whatever we may think of Ben Gurion, whether or not we agree with his economic and political theories, one thing we must admit, he is a very great man, he has a most unusual mind, and he has a vast amount of knowledge, not only of Jewish history and lore but also of world culture. He is a remarkable personality. He has his faults, as have all great leaders, and he may not always be as diplomatic as some of us would like, but he knows the Jewish tradition; he knows the Bible as well as many a Biblical scholar. He knows the background of the Bible, the history of the Bible, the philosophy of the Bible, and the deeper meaning of each word of the Bible. And he knows the Rabbinic tradition as well. And when

7) Ketubot, 110b.

he wants to quote from our classic sources, he knows what to quote. That is the brilliance of Ben Gurion. His words are worthy of close study.

When Ben Gurion keeps pleading for *aliyah*, for the immigration, especially of American Jews, Western Jews, it is not only because of his interest in Israel, not only because Israel needs these Jews. It is true that Israel does need the American Jew with his know-how, with his advanced knowledge and education. You cannot develop a country solely on the experience of the Oriental Jews, the Jews who came from the Arab countries. And so naturally he wants *aliyah* for Israel's sake. But when he emphasizes *aliyah* it is also because he is afraid of the *galut*, and of what the *galut* can mean to the Jew.

He cannot, of course, speak to the Jews in the Soviet countries. There, the hour is now too late. He is still hopeful that some day there will be a change; and when the change occurs, there will be a tremendous flood of immigration. He has no doubt about it. But now they cannot leave; it is too late. Khrushchev does not permit them to leave, so Ben Gurion cannot speak to them. But he is also afraid of what is happening to us American Jews. He knows the dangers of assimilation. And he knows what happened to the Jews in Egypt where they also lived at first in an atmosphere of brotherhood and tolerance. Ben Gurion knows *both* possible consequences of "living in Egypt." He sees in Russia actual enslavement of the body but in the Western countries he sees a spiritual bondage, what Achad Ha-am called *avdut b'cherut*, slavery in freedom.

One can be a slave even in freedom, one can be spiritually in bondage. And that is what worries Ben Gurion. He is not at all impressed by what we call the present revival of Jewish religious life in America. He knows that million-dollar synagogues are being built throughout the country but he also knows that many of these synagogues are almost empty throughout the year, except on the High Holy Days. He knows that parents are sending their children to Hebrew Schools, but he also knows that immediately after Bar Mitzvah, eighty per cent of these children terminate their instruction and soon forget what they have learned. And he also is aware of the great ignorance that many American Jews have in matters pertaining to Judaism. He knows all that, and he is concerned. He knows especially the influence of the environment. After all, we are a minority living amidst a Christian civilization. He knows it, and he is worried about it.

This is why he keeps pounding and pounding away for *aliyah*. If one wants a full Jewish life, a full religious life, more easily and naturally, then Ben Gurion is correct. In Israel they do not need to battle for it as we have to battle for it here. And so when he quoted that passage of the Talmud, it was not merely to taunt the pious American Jews who criticize what is going on in Israel. He quoted that Talmudic passage because it reveals a great truth. I know that many American Rabbis tried to apologize in their sermons for that statement in the Talmud; they have tried to explain it away; but the truth is just as the Talmud states it and the truth is the way Ben Gurion understood it. And please do not say that it is merely a solitary statement by a single Rabbi, a sort of *obiter dictum,* just a passing remark. No! The statement begins with the words: *Tanu rabbanan,* "The Rabbis have taught." It is not just one Rabbi who said it. *Tanu rabbanan* means that the majority of the Rabbis have taught it. It was an accepted decision by the Rabbis, because it speaks the truth as they saw it. The statement is: "Any Jew who lives outside of the land of Israel, *domeh kmi, is like one* who has no God."

The Rabbis immediately question their own statement: "Have we a right to say that any Jew who does not live in *Eretz Yisrael* has no God?"[8] Of course not; God is everywhere. But it does not say, "he has no God." It says, *domah kmi,*

8) *Ibid.*

"he is *like one* who has no God." He has a God, but his God
is not completely his. His is not a God who reigns supreme in
his environment. The Rabbis tried to explain it further: "It
is like one who was participating in strange worship."[9] And we
are participating in strange worship. All you have to do is to
turn on your radio or television at this time of the year — at
Easter and also at Christmas — and you will understand what
the Rabbis meant. We have a God, but it is not our God who
influences the life in the environment that is ours. Turn to any
channel today or tomorrow on your television and your
children will see plays with the Christ story, or turn to any
station on the radio and the Easter message will be pounded
into your ears. We are under the influence of that environment. While we have a God, *domeh kmi sh'en lo eloha*, "it is
like one who has no God," because He is not the primary influence in our lives. And that is why the Rabbis continued:
"But one who lives in the land of Israel, *domeh kmi sh'yesh
lo eloha*, "he is *like one* who has a God." In Israel the Jew leads
a different life. He may not even be religious, but he cannot
help being influenced by his religion because his environment there is Jewish and religious. Wherever he turns, there is
Jewishness surrounding him. The atmosphere is Jewish, and
that is why Jewish life is assured because it is the Jewish God
who plays the important role.

You recall, perhaps, an anecdote that is told about the late
Chief Rabbi Kook, of blessed memory. He was very tolerant,
as you know, towards the *chalutzim*, even to the irreligious
chalutzim. He befriended them. The story is told that an
American group of orthodox Jews came on a tour to Israel
and were received by Rabbi Kook. One of these Jews taunted
Rabbi Kook, saying: "Rabbi Kook, you are such a pious
leader, and we look up to you. How can you be so friendly to
these *chalutzim*, many of whom are so irreligious?" And Rabbi Kook replied: "My friend, it hurts me too that they are not

9) *Ibid.*

religious. I would like to see them observant of our religious precepts, and I am trying my best to show them the beauty of our religion. But there is one thing of which I am certain; I am confident that the grandchildren of these *chalutzim* will remain Jews. I am not so confident about your grandchildren." And Rabbi Kook spoke a deep truth in these words.

We know that in America there cannot be that condition of enslavement which our brethren are experiencing in Russia today. We have faith in America and in America's loyalty to democracy and human freedom. America would no longer be America if she forsook her ideals of democracy. And we are confident that the Jewish position in America is absolutely safe and assured physically. But we should be worried about something else, we should give serious thought to Ben Gurion's warning concerning the dangers of assimilation.

It is very interesting, too, that in that same page in the Talmud where the statement quoted by Ben Gurion is made, there is another statement in the name of Rabbi Judah. True, not *tanu rabbanan*, not by the majority of the Rabbis, but a single opinion that nevertheless has validity. Said Rabbi Judah: "A Jew who lives in Babylon, *k'ilu dar b'eretz Yisrael*, may be regarded as if he were to live in Israel."[10] That is the only place in the Rabbinic literature where some semblance of equality to Israel is conferred on another land, Babylon.

This exception is made by Rabbi Judah because in Babylon there was no danger of assimilation. The Jews there developed a remarkable Jewish life with great academies of learning. In that land the great Rabbis were produced, the creators of the Talmud. Even the ordinary Jews, the farmers, the workingmen, would stop their work twice a year, for a month at a time, to assemble at a *kallah*, a popular seminar, where the Rabbis would teach them the Law. Such Jewish cultural and spiritual richness was developed in Babylon that the Rabbis felt Jewish life was safeguarded, almost as assured there as it would be in

10) *Ibid.*

Palestine. That is the reason that Rabbi Judah prohibited a
Jew from leaving Babylon for any other part of the world. But
this same Rabbi Judah also said that "if one lives in the land
of Israel he dare not leave it,"[11] so great was his love for *Eretz
Yisrael*.

And so, to conclude all that I have tried to say to you: when
we refuse to listen to the call of Ben Gurion and to all the
Jews in Israel who echo his plea, let us be honest with ourselves.
Let us not try to rationalize our actions deceptively. Let us
admit that we prefer to remain in our adopted land because
we like it here. We prefer to live in America. What hurts Ben
Gurion is that we try to justify our remaining in the diaspora
with complex intellectual arguments. Let us admit honestly
that we are happy here.

But if we do prefer to be here, let us recognize the challenge
and the warning that Ben Gurion hurls at us. Let us realize
that we are a minority, that we are living in a Christian environment and that there is the danger and likelihood of assimilation. If the process of assimilation continues with growing
force, and if the resistance to assimilation becomes weaker,
then we are lost. If we want to answer Ben Gurion effectively,
we have to strengthen our resistance to assimilation, the resistance of our children, the resistance of our grandchildren; we
have to work and work, plan and plan, make sacrifice after
sacrifice, to build spiritual and cultural fortresses, synagogues
and schools, Seminaries and Yeshivot, libraries and academies; we have to foster more learning and scholarship. If we
do this and thereby create a healthy resistance to the dangers
of assimilation, then, without justifying our remaining in *galut*,
we shall be able in some measure, to truly paraphrase Rabbi
Judah's statement about the Jews in Babylon, by saying that
"the Jews who live in America are like the Jews who live in
Eretz Israel."

11) *Ibid.*

Portrait
of a Rabbi

A SON'S TRIBUTE TO A BELOVED FATHER

Preached Friday evening, October 31, 1952 in memory of
the author's father, Rabbi Bernard L. Levinthal, who died
September 23, 1952. Parts of this discourse had also been
delivered at a Memorial Meeting, held at Bnai Abraham
Synagogue in Philadelphia, October 23, 1952.

I think you can well understand how difficult it is for me to
speak on the theme that I have selected for my discourse this
Sabbath eve. The feelings of my heart at this time may best
be described by the words of Rabbi Judah the Saint, uttered
at the death of Emperor Antonius, to whom he had been closely bound in friendship and regard: *Nitpardah chavilah*, "The
cord which tied us together has been torn asunder."[1]

My father's relationship to me, as well as to the other children in our family, and his influence upon us, are vividly illustrated by a beautiful comment of the Rabbis. Referring to
the scene portrayed in the Bible, which tells how God spoke to
Moses from the burning bush,[2] the sages ask: "In what form
did God reveal Himself to Moses?" And they answer: *Nigleh
alav bkolo shel aviv*, "He revealed Himself to him in the voice
of his own father."[3] That is the secret of father's great influence upon us; when he spoke to us, we heard, as it were, God
speaking to us.

To us, his children, he was the *kohen hagadol me'echav*,

1) Abodah Zarah, 10b.
2) Exodus, 3:4 f.
3) Exodus Rabbah, 3:1.

169

"the priest that is highest among his brethren";[4] and we took sspecial pride that, as the Rabbis interpreted that phrase, *gadlehu mishel echav*, "his greatness was recognized by his fellow priests,"[5] his colleagues in the American Rabbinate. This is not the biased opinion of a devoted son thinking of his father, but the virtually unanimous opinion of the American Rabbis, especially in the orthodox group, who had been privileged to know him.

Pursuing their comments on this Biblical phrase, the Rabbis enumerate the qualities which the High Priest had to possess in order that his greatness should not only outweigh that of his fellow priests but also win the recognition of his colleagues: *sheyehe gadol me'echav b'noy, b'chakmah, b'osher, b'koach*, "He had to be greater than his colleagues in handsomeness, in wisdom, in wealth, in strength."[6] Father was heavenly endowed with these gifts.

Gadol me'echav b'noy. "He was to be great in handsomeness." Father possessed a handsome appearance. It was not the handsomeness of motion-picture standards, but a strikingness in his appearance that immediately made you aware that you were standing in the presence of a great man. When he entered a bus or subway, all eyes would instantly be fixed upon him. There was a famous photographer in Philadelphia in my boyhood days, by the name of Gutekunst whose photographic studies won him national fame and recognition. I recall an interview reported in the Philadelphia press, in which he had been asked: "Who was the most striking figure that you have photographed?" And he answered: "The two heads that were the most striking, and a photographer's delight, were those of Judge Mayer Sulzberger and of Rabbi B. L. Levinthal." His sparkling eyes, his broad forehead, his silver locks,

4) Leviticus, 21:10.
5) Yoma, 18a.
6) *Ibid.*, see Torah Temimah on this verse, note 64, for other references with variations of qualities required.

made him what the Rabbis defined as: *adam shel tzurah*, "the man distinguished in appearance."[7] There was an intellectual and spiritual halo about him which immediately captivated your attention.

In the crucial year, 1939, when Great Britain issued the White Paper on Palestine — curtailing the rights of the Jewish people in Palestine — a delegation of America's outstanding Jewish leaders was appointed to meet with Secretary of State Cordell Hull, to beseech him to intercede and urge Britain to annul that harmful instrument. Needless to say that the most distinguished Jews of America made up that illustrious group. Father was designated a member of that delegation to represent the Orthodox Jews of America. At the end of the interview, Secretary Hull left his desk, and, as if mystically drawn to father, walked over to him and said: "Rabbi, confer upon me your blessing." Father, in the midst of the hushed and reverent silence of all present, pronounced upon the bowed head of Secretary Hull the Priestly Benediction.

Gadol b'chakmah, "He was to be great in wisdom." Father was bountifully endowed with this great gift. His was not only the wisdom of learning — the mastery of the Torah in its broadest sense — but also the wisdom of intelligence, the mastery of understanding man and man's every-day problems. Daily there was a constant procession of men and women who came to him for advice to help them in their trials, troubles, and tribulations. Businessmen with claims against each other, instead of seeking redress in the civil courts, would beseech him to act as arbiter between them. He was known by all as a *pike'ach*, a Hebrew word difficult to translate because it includes so much, a man with keenness of mind, with quickness to grasp what another wants to express, with sharpness to penetrate the justice or injustice of one's claim.

It was this gift of *gadol b'chakmah* that endeared him not

7) Taanit, 16a.

only to the members of his own Orthodox group but to Jews
of all other groups as well, even the radicals and anti-reli-
gionists.

As for the third quality, *gadol b'osher*, "greatness in wealth,"
father was certainly not great in monetary wealth. Those were
the pioneering years in America for the Orthodox Rabbinate,
and struggle for the daily livelihood was the common lot of
everyone of them. But he was rich in all the qualities essential
for great and fruitful spiritual leadership. He was a constant
student, ever eager to enrich further his mind with Jewish learning and scholarship. He possessed a phenomenal memory, so
that, like Rabbi Eliezer, son of Hyrcanos, his mind was "a
cemented cistern which loses not a drop."[8] He was a remarkable preacher and public speaker, whose brilliant interpretations of Biblical and Rabbinic texts fascinated an audience
and held them spellbound for hours. And he was a skillful
organizer, the fruits of whose work still bless the life of the
Philadelphia Jewish community. Aye, he was great in the
wealth of his endowed gifts of mind and heart.

Called to the Rabbinate in Philadelphia in 1891, he found
the community almost a wilderness in Jewish life. He organized the first Talmud Torah, a Hebrew school for the young;
he founded the *Vaad Hakashrut*, the body supervising the
kashrut or ritual requirements of food; he was the inspirer of
the first Zionist Society in that city, and one of the original
organizers of the Federation of American Zionists. Many other organizations and societies which served the needs of that
early community, and which serve it to this very day, came into
being because of his influence and his activity.

And as for the fourth requirement, *gadol b'koach*, "greatness in strength," the Rabbis of course did not refer to physical strength alone, though father must have been blessed with
such *koach*, for he violated all the modern health rules. He

8) Abot, 2:8.

seldom ate at regular hours. If he were immersed in some conversation, or busy at some task, hours could go by before he would respond to mother's pleadings to have his meal. He hardly ever retired before long after midnight. He was constantly rushing from one meeting to another, from one conference to another. There was a driving force within him; he seldom relaxed. Thank God, his body was able to withstand such physical and nervous strain so that he lived to a ripe old age.

But he also possessed what the Rabbis had in mind in that phrase, great spiritual and moral strength. He had lofty ideals of Rabbinic service, instilled within him by generations of ancestors, great Rabbinic leaders. And he had the spiritual strength to uphold these ideals despite all odds. At a time when Zionism was fought by many Rabbis, even of the orthodox group, he was among the first to espouse the Zionist cause and to enlist in its service. In the early years of his Rabbinate socialism and radicalism were popular among the masses of the people. Many viewed religion as the great opponent of the working man and as the apologist for the economic status quo. There was in Philadelphia at that time a fine and active society known as the Hebrew Literature Society. A Public Forum was there established which met weekly to discuss current and cultural problems. The direction of this Forum was in the hands of a radical group. As a courtesy to father, they invited him to be one of the lecturers, though they felt certain that he would refuse. However, he accepted, and gave a series of talks on "Labor Laws in the Talmud." During the question and discussion period that always followed the lecture, the crowded audience of men and women were eager to see and hear the challenges of those waiting to heckle him. But father stood his ground till long after midnight, receiving an ovation even from those who differed from him. It is interesting to note that many of those who were vociferous in their denunciation of religion soon became father's devoted admirers and friends and also turned into some of the most active workers in Jewish communal causes.

Father was never parochial or narrow in his attitude to Jewish life. All Jews were his concern. Like the High Priest of old who, we are told, had to wear *al libo*, "on his heart,"[9] the breastplate of judgment, on which were inscribed the names of all the twelve tribes, so father bore on his heart the interests of all groups among the Jewish people. Nay, more, it was not enough for the High Priest to bear the names of all the tribes on his heart. He had to bear these names also "on his shoulders,"[10] to carry the burdens of all the tribes and to work for the interests of all of them. Father, true high priest that he was, carried the welfare of all his people on his shoulders as well as on his heart.

There was an additional gift that father possessed. The ancient Rabbis, in a strange statement, assert that: "two hundred of the heads of the Sanhedrin — the Court of Justice in Jerusalem — were of the tribe of Issakor."[11] It is an interesting comment deserving of deeper study. Surely, they did not intend that these words be taken seriously, for, at the time of the Rabbis and the existence of the Sanhedrin, the ten tribes — including Issakar — were lost, and no one could trace a person's genealogy to that tribe. The words were to be understood figuratively. The tribe of Issakar was distinguished by one great quality, for the patriarch Jacob, in blessing his sons, referred to this when he said of Issakar, "And he bowed his shoulder to bear, and became a servant under task-work,"[12] which the Rabbis interpret as "bearing on their shoulders the *ole ha-Torah*, the yoke, the burden of the Torah."[13] They were to be the scholars among the people and the ones to bear the

9) Exodus, 28:29.
10) *Ibid.*, v. 9, 12.
11) Genesis Rabbah, 98:17; 72:5.
12) Genesis, 49:15.
13) Genesis Rabbah, 98:12.

burden of making the Torah the inheritance of the Jewish people.

The Bible gives a further description of the members of this tribe: "And the sons of Issakar knowing *binah la'itim*, the understanding of the times, to know what Israel ought to do."[14] They had not only learning, but also an understanding of the times in which they lived. They knew the demands of the new age that had to be considered.

Father could indeed be characterized as a true member of the tribe of Issakar. He had a keen appreciation of the changed times in America in which Jewish life found itself, and of what these changes demanded of Jewish leaders.

Today, late Friday night lecture services are in vogue in most synagogues. We generally think of this innovation in our religious life as a product of the Conservative or Reform groups. However, already at the beginning of the century, father had instituted a series of regular weekly Friday night lectures throughout the fall and winter seasons, which he delivered at Touro Hall, at Tenth and Carpenter streets in Philadelphia. Despite the fact that the building was far from the Jewish section of the city, indeed, it was in the heart of an Italian immigrant area, the large auditorium was crowded to overflowing every Friday eve with men and women who hungered for a Jewish message that gave them a new understanding of their rich cultural and spiritual heritage. There was no music, no singing, no religious service at these gatherings; but his inspiring discourses, by the richness of thought and learning that they revealed, had the power to attract large and enthusiastic audiences of both old and young.

So, too, father was concerned about those Jewish lads attending the public High Schools who did not continue their Hebrew studies. Singlehandedly, he organized a Hebrew High School, which met in our home several evenings a week. He

14) I Chronicles, 12:32.

himself taught Talmud to the students. He enlisted an excellent Hebraist, a Dr. Hess, as a volunteer teacher of Hebrew; and he invited Dr. Menachem Eichler — mind you — a Conservative Rabbi, to teach Jewish history. It was a fine group of youngsters, the choicest of the community's youth, who joined this class. A number of them later entered the Jewish Theological Seminary and the Yeshivah Rabbi Isaac Elchanan to study for the Rabbinate, and some became, and to this day are, lay leaders in the Jewish communal life of Philadelphia.

It was this appreciation of the demands of the new age — "to know what Israel ought to do" — that moved father to become one of the leaders among the founders of the Rabbi Isaac Elchanan Yeshivah — later to become Yeshivah University — so as to meet the new requirements essential for the Orthodox Rabbinate in America. It was he who insisted that the leadership of the Yeshivah be conferred upon a man who combined rich Jewish learning with modern scholarship. Both the late president, Dr. Bernard Revel, and the present president, Dr. Samuel Belkin, were suggested by him as men meeting these requirements.

Many of the old Rabbis who came to America in the early years of father's Rabbinate, relate that before leaving the old country they would travel to call on Rabbi Isaac Elchanan of Kovno — then the recognized Rabbinic leader of his age — to bid farewell and to ask for his blessing for the new life which they would encounter. Invariably, they tell, the old sage would say to them: "Go to see Rabbi Levinthal in Philadelphia. He will advise you how to meet your rabbinic problems in the new world." And the fact is that there was hardly a Rabbi of the old school — whether or not he received that advice — who did not, on his arrival in America, visit father and look to him for guidance in his new tasks.

Father remained faithful to the old — the old tradition, the old ideals — but was not blind to the changes of the new world. With reference to the farewell admonition of Moses to his people: "Remember the days of old, *binu shnot dor vador*, "understand the years of many generations,"[15] there is an interesting comment attributed to one of the latter-day sages, which says: "Read not *shnot* as *years*, but as *shonot*, "changes." What Moses instructed his people was really: "Remember the days of old, but understand the *changes* of every generation!"

This was the admonition which father followed, and which won for him the esteem of Jews of all views. Even those who differed with him in ideology recognized him as one who understood them and who appreciated their efforts to assure, in their own way, the furtherance of Jewish life in America.

Above all, father had faith in the future of Jewish life in this land. One of the senior leaders in the Orthodox Jewish group — Rabbi Eliezer Silver of Cincinnati — in his eulogy at father's funeral, mentioned that, on his arrival in America a number of decades ago, he had called on father and expressed his great disappointment at finding here such little pursuit of Talmudic learning, especially among the young, which meant to him the eventual disappearance from American Jewry of that classic wisdom. "Be patient," he remembered father had said to him, "you and I will yet see ten thousand young men studying Talmud in this land!" Both lived to see that prediction more than fulfilled. Father had the faith and conviction that Judaism could and would live and thrive in America, because he had the faith that the American Jew would want it to live!

We are grateful to God that father lived to a ripe old age — that he passed the age of *gevurah*, of strength, which the Rabbis designated the eightieth year in one's life.[16] Until three or four years before his death he was in full activity, guiding and inspiring his people. The last few years were sad for him, not

15) Deuteronomy, 32:7.
16) Abot, 5:21.

because he was in pain or bedridden, but because he realized that he could no longer serve the people whom he loved. "Note," say the Rabbis, "that throughout all his life David is always referred to as *king,* as it is written: 'And the king David was old,' but as he approached his death, the Bible no longer speaks of him as *king,* as it is written: 'And the days of David drew nigh that he should die.' "[17] Throughout the sixty-one years of father's ministry in Philadelphia, people always knew him as Rabbi Levinthal. Alas, he was saddened, as David must similarly have been, that, as he approached his end, he could not serve and act as the Rabbi of his people.

But such men do not die. As the Rabbis note: *Tzadikim b'mitatam kruyin chayim,* "The righteous even in their death are called alive!"[18] So, too, we may say of this High Priest among his brethren: His days have come to an end, but he lives and will continue to live in the grateful hearts of a people whom he served with all his heart, with all his soul, and with all his might.

17) Genesis Rabbah, 96:3; Deuteronomy Rabbah, 9:3; I Kings, 1:1; 2:1.
18) Berakot, 18a.

Ideals
for the Rabbinate

Response delivered at the joint celebration of the 35th anniversary of both the founding of the Brooklyn Jewish
Center and the author's Rabbinate at the Center, November 22, 1954.

Our ancient Rabbis teach us that when we approach God in
prayer or in petition we should join our supplication with
words of *shevach v'hodayah*, praise and thankfulness.[1] In the
spirit of that injunction, I, too, wish to begin my remarks
with words of *shevach v'hodayah*.

I am thankful to God that He has granted me life and
permitted me to celebrate with you this happy anniversary of
thirty-five years of joint service in behalf of our faith and our
people. Fervently do I offer that ancient benediction, so beautifully sung for us this evening by that heavenly-endowed
singer, Richard Tucker, thanking God *shehecheyanu, v'ki-*
yemanu, v'higianu lazman hazeh.

I am thankful to our Heavenly Father that I am blessed to
have with me at this celebration my beloved wife and help-
mate in my work through these many years. It is often said
that it is hard to be a Rabbi. I want to assure you that it is
even harder to be a *Rebbetzin*. And I am thankful that I am
able to attest that Mrs. Levinthal has carried her share of the
Rabbinate — the role of *Rebbetzin* — with dignity, with intelligence, and with that rare quality, *sekhel* — good common
sense. God grant that I may be able to celebrate together with

1) Berakot, 32a.

179

her and our beloved children many joyous occasions in the future.

I am thankful also that we have with us so many of the old members, the original founders, builders and organizers of our beloved institution. Many, alas, are gone, and we miss them greatly. Their memories are deeply enshrined within our hearts. But we are thankful for those still in our midst; and we pray that they may continue to be with us, and work with us, for many years to come.

And I am thankful to all of you, dear friends, for your friendship, your affection, and your cooperation in all the thirty-five years of our Center's activity. God grant that we may be privileged to continue that relationship for a long time to come.

My friends, this is a double celebration, the thirty-fifth anniversary of the founding of our beloved Center, and the thirty-fifth anniversary of my own Rabbinate here. Now, according to the Rabbis, *en m'arvin simchah b'simchah,* "we are not to combine two happy celebrations."[2] The Rabbis felt that there are so few truly joyous events in one's life that we should celebrate each one separately. But in essence, this is only one celebration; they are two that are really one. A Rabbi without a congregation is like a soul without a body — he cannot truly function. And a congregation without a Rabbi is a body without a soul, also unable to perform its true function. It was our good fortune that at the very birth of the Center the *guf* found its *neshamah,* and the *neshamah* found its *guf.* And I think we can say in all sincerity that it was a *zivug,* a union, made in heaven, and therefore was a *zivug oleh l'yafeh,* a union that rose to beauty and to glory.

Thirty-five years in Rabbinic service is a long time. Indeed, my own Rabbinate had begun here in Brooklyn nine years before I came to the Center. You may ask in wonderment:

2) Mo'ed Katan, 8b.

"Forty-four years in the Rabbinate — a leader among Jews — how could you endure so long, and yet retain (what I hope I shall continue to possess) a smile and a spirit of youthfulness?" The Talmud records a similar question posed to a famous sage, Rabbi Eleazer, the son of Shammua, old and many years in the service of his people. *Bameh he'erakta yamim*, "How did you succeed in achieving old age; how did you endure so long a service in spiritual leadership?" And the old Rabbi's answer is very significant. "In all my years I never made the Synagogue *kopandaria*, a short cut." It was prohibited to use a synagogue as a short-cut to reach a desired destination, and the Rabbi attests that he never violated that precept. "I have never stepped over the heads of my people — a holy people," he continued. In ancient times the students sat on the floor and the Rabbi or teacher sat on a chair before the lectern; and the Rabbi declared that even when the floor was crowded, he never walked over the heads of his disciples, for, to him, they were all a holy people. And lastly, he said: "I have never raised my hands in priestly benediction without uttering the words, 'to bless His people Israel *b'ahavah*, with love.' "[3]

In all humility, I would answer this question, if put to me, in exactly the same words: In all my years, I have never made the synagogue a short-cut to achieve fame or success in other fields; I have never utilized the synagogue as a means to reach other goals. To me, the synagogue has been an end in itself, worthy of all my endeavors, of all the capacities that I may possess. The synagogue has been the all-pervasive instrument through which I could best serve my people, my country, my God.

And, like Rabbi Eleazar, I too would say: "In all my years, I have never walked over the heads of my people — a holy people." I have never forced my opinions upon my people; I have

3) Megillah, 27b.

always respected the opinions of every Jew, no matter in what humble position he was, for, to me, every Jew is part of a holy people. I have held strong opinions and convictions of my own, but I would not force them upon my people. I would argue, I would reason, I would endeavor to persuade through logic and argument; I would always try to see the truth and the validity in the arguments and opinions of others. Even when I had the power to force my opinions upon others, I never did so, because, like Rabbi Eleazar, I refused to step over the heads of my people.

And finally, I may say in all sincerity, I never raised my hands in the service of my people without thinking of the words, "to bless His people *b'ahavah*, with love." There has been a great and unbounded love for my people in my heart, and that love has inspired me in all my endeavors. When you love someone, no task is too great or too difficult to perform in his behalf, and it is this love for my people that has made my work so easy, my heaviest task so light, in all these many years. Not that I have been blind to my people's faults nor to the failings of my congregation. There were times when I had to reprove and to reproach my people; but even then I did so *b'ahavah*, with love, as a loving father reproves a wayward child. This is the answer to the question *bameh he'erakta yamim*; this is the secret of whatever success my humble efforts have attained.

It is not for me to record here the blessed achievements of our Center. Others have already done so most eloquently. But if I were to summarize in one word what these thirty-five years have meant, I would put it in the Hebrew letters denoting the number 35 — *lamed* and *he* — which together spell *"for God!"* These thirty-five years have been dedicated to bring godliness into our lives, into the life of our community, our people, our country, into our strivings for all mankind.

My friends, it is good to celebrate the accomplishments of the past; ours is indeed a glorious past. We were the pioneers in the effort to revitalize the synagogue in our American-Jewish life; we played a leading role in achieving the rebirth of Israel and Israel's land; and we have done much to revivify Jewish life and thought not only in our own community but also throughout the land.

But we dare not concentrate our thoughts on the past alone. Tonight the accent must be on the future. Our Rabbis, in a striking comment, remind us that wherever in the Bible the emphasis is on the word *vayehi*, *"and it was"* — in the past — *eno ela lashon tzarah*, "there it bespeaks tragedy." But wherever the emphasis is on the word *v'hayah*, *"and it shall be"* — in the future — *eno elo·lashon simchah*, "there it bespeaks joy!"[4] Tonight, the emphasis of our celebration must be on *v'hayah*, the future. We must dedicate ourselves anew to the great tasks that lie before us. Let us re-consecrate ourselves, in the spirit of consecration that filled the hearts of the founders and builders of our institution thirty-five years ago, so that the future of our Center may be even greater and more glorious than was its past. Let us resolve tonight to strive to bring closer that glorious *v'hayah* which the prophet foretold, "And it shall be that the Lord shall be ruler over all the earth,"[5] when all mankind shall live according to His law, the law of truth and justice, of love and mercy, of peace and brotherhood.

4) Esther Rabbah, beginning; Leviticus Rabbah, 11:7.
5) Zakariah, 14:9.

The Garments
of the Priest

Response delivered at a celebration in honor
of the author's 70th birthday,
at the Brooklyn Jewish Center, May 4, 1958.

My heart overflows with gratitude in this hour. Gratitude, first of all, to our Father in Heaven for having granted me life, for having preserved me, and for having enabled me to celebrate this milestone in my life — my seventieth birthday. And I am grateful beyond words to God for permitting me to have the love of my youth, my life companion — my beloved wife — sharing with me the joy of this hour. Whenever I think of our relationship I am reminded of the very beautiful tribute that a great Hebrew writer in America, Maximon, once said about the wife of a prominent man in public life: "The wife of a public man may be compared to the accompanist of a soloist. When you hear a soloist, a singer or musician, all your thoughts are concentrated upon him; you do not take any notice at all of the accompanist, and yet the accompanist plays a very important role. One false note of the accompanist and the entire performance would be spoiled." I am thankful to God that He blessed me with a fine accompanist.

I am also grateful to God that my seventieth birthday coincides with the tenth anniversary of the birth of the State of Israel. My heart had yearned for Zion Reborn ever since my childhood. That I lived to see the fulfillment of this dream gives me the greatest happiness.

And, of course, I am thankful to you, my friends in this

congregation, who have worked with me all these years in the magnificent endeavor to establish here this citadel of our faith.

Now, my friends, many nice things have been said about me tonight by the speakers, but I am now old enough not to be spoiled by all I have heard. Jews are a merciful and kind people, they have good hearts. And much that was said came from the goodness and generosity of the speakers' hearts. I think I can, however, in all sincerity, say this about myself and about my Rabbinate — and I say this without boasting and without conceit — that I have always tried to do my best. I have at all times set before me a very lofty ideal of the Rabbinate. I may not have always attained my high resolves, but I tried nevertheless.

There is a very interesting comment of the Rabbis on a simple sentence that we read yesterday in the Torah lesson. It deals with the garments of the high priest and how he was to dress when he entered the Sanctuary to perform the holy service. The Bible says: *bezot yavo Aharon el hakodesh*, "in this fashion shall Aaron enter the Sanctuary." And then it proceeds to say, "He shall be garbed with a tunic, a garment of linen, and breeches of linen, and a girdle of linen, and a mitre of linen."[1] When the Rabbis read this verse they were quite astonished. The Bible is very sparing in language, and yet here in one sentence it uses the word *bod*, linen, four times. It could just as well have said, "All the garments shall be of linen." And so they asked in the Talmud: "Four times the word *bod*. Why?" There is an answer, they say. "It is to teach the priests that the garments had to be made of the choicest of linen."[2] Not just ordinary linen — it had to be of the choicest linen. I believe, my friends, that what the Rabbis had in mind was not only the material garments that the priests wore

1) Leviticus, 16:3, 4.
2) Yoma, 35a.

but also the spiritual garments of the priests. These, too, had
to be of the choicest quality.

That is the ideal that I set for myself. I have always sought
to attain the choicest of spiritual garments. In whatever I did,
in whatever humble piece of work I had to do, I always envi-
sioned a high standard.

In my preaching, I have always worried. To this day, people will say to me, "You, worrying now, after so many years
of preaching?" Let me confess to you — I am a nervous wreck
every time I have to preach. I worry when I prepare the sermon.
I cannot always reach the heights I would like, to which my
congregation is entitled. I worry while preaching lest I may not
have achieved the best. Even after I have finished preaching
and the congregation is gracious enough to give me a *yasher
koach*, to congratulate me, I go home still worrying — it
should have been better! And I say this with all sincerity,
whatever modest success I have achieved has been due primarily, as I evaluate myself, to this urge to maintain a high
standard of achievement.

Now, at this age, dear friends, one likes to reminisce, to
look back. And as I look back upon my years and upon my
Rabbinate, two things stand out foremost in my mind. First,
that I have always been associated with Brooklyn. Mrs. Levinthal often teases me, jokingly of course, when we hear of
other Rabbis who change their positions, going from west to
east, north to south, she says to me: "These Rabbis see the
country. You came to Brooklyn and you stayed in Brooklyn."
That is the truth, dear friends. When I entered the Seminary,
in 1906, as a freshman, Professor Schechter, of blessed memory, assigned the students to small posts for practice preaching. Some students were assigned to Connecticut, some to
New Jersey, others to Philadelphia; I was assigned to Brooklyn,
to a little synagogue on Wyona Street in East New York. I was
there two years and then I received some kind of promotion.
I went to a little larger congregation, again in Brooklyn, in

the Greenpoint section on Noble Street. And when I graduated in 1910 I received a call, once more in Brooklyn, in South Brooklyn, on 9th Street. Then in 1915 I received another call, still in Brooklyn, to Petach Tikvah, in this very section. And then came the blessed year, 1919, in which I became wedded, as it were, to the Brooklyn Jewish Center.

The second thing that stands out in my mind is that I always had to start from the beginning. I was a kind of *chalutz*, a pioneer. I sometimes envy the men who enter the Rabbinate today. They generally go to established congregations, completely organized and well-functioning, no debts, no mortgages, no notes. In my first student position on Wyona Street, when Yom Kippur came, I was asked to make an appeal for a building fund. They wanted to erect a larger synagogue — and they did, on Jamaica Avenue — Temple Sinai. I was only one or two years in my first regular position on 9th Street, when an enterprising company purchased the synagogue building. The congregation was thus forced to erect a new synagogue, and it had to be a larger one, with a bigger mortgage and more debts. During the years that I was there a good part of my ministry had to be channeled towards clearing the indebtedness. Congregation Petach Tikvah was a new organization when I came to it. Its building was not yet finished when I arrived for Rosh Hashanah. There, too, throughout the time I was there, the words I heard most frequently were "mortgages" and "notes"; I almost became a banker.

When finally, in 1919, I became the Rabbi of the Brooklyn Jewish Center, all that we had was an office near Albany Avenue. Not one spadeful of earth had been dug. We started from the beginning. As a matter of fact, the entire venture was then only a dream. It was because I had faith in the realization of that dream that I accepted the call. But again, for years, you can imagine what I had to do — help in the task of securing money to pay the congregation's debts. We went through the years of depression, and what horrible years they were. We required tremendous strength in order to continue our work. I was a real *chalutz*, just like the early *chalutzim* in *Eretz Yisrael*. And we had not only the task of erecting a building; we had to build Jewish minds. It was not like today, when Jews want to join the synagogue. Today, in all the new suburbs, as soon as a few Jews settle, they build a synagogue. Every Jew feels that he must join the synagogue. In those early years, on bended knees we had to plead with Jews to join the synagogue. I remember how hard I had to urge parents to send their children to the Hebrew School. Today it is easy. How I envy the young men who leave the Seminary today! We had to build Jewish hearts and Jewish minds. And so you can understand, dear friends, that at seventy, I should feel a little tired.

Now the Rabbis beautifully characterized the various ages of a man. When one is sixty, he has already reached *ziknah*, old age. When he is seventy, he attains *sevah*, the hoary head.[3] I became gray at a very young age. I had the signs of *sevah* before I was forty. For many years I could say, as Rabbi Eleazar ben Azariah said, "I am *like* a man of seventy."[4] But today it is no longer *k'ben shivim, like* a man of seventy, but actually *ben shivim!* There is a great difference between the two phrases. At seventy one begins to feel that "the day is short," and that it is getting shorter — "and the work is still great."[5] I can, in all sincerity, say that I still would like to work and that I still can work. Naturally, I should want to be relieved of much of the physical labor, the routine work.

At one of the celebrations on my fiftieth birthday, I spoke of two functionaries who had served in the temple in ancient times, the *Kohen*, the priest, and the *Levite*. The Bible expressly says that the *Levite* is to work only to his fiftieth year. "And from the age of fifty years they shall return from

3) Abot, 5:24.
4) Berakot, 28a.
5) Cf. Abot, 2:20.

the service of the work, and shall serve no more."[6] He was to be relieved of all work when he reached his fiftieth year. But of the *Kohen*, you will not find in the Bible any mention of his retirement. Why the distinction? The answer is very simple. The *Levite* had to do manual work; he had to take care of the physical condition of the sanctuary; "every one that entered in to do the work of service, and the work of bearing burdens in the tent of meeting."[7] When he reached fifty years, the ancients felt, a younger man should do this physical work. But of the priest it is said: "for the lips of the priest should keep knowledge, and from his mouth they should seek Torah."[8] That is not manual labor. It is the labor of the mind; and the older one gets, the more does the mind become enriched. The tragedy of the American Rabbinate — the reason we have so many Rabbis Emeriti — is that the Rabbi has to be not only the *Kohen* but the *Levite* as well. He is so preoccupied with actual physical duties that both his mind and his body become physically exhausted.

I should like to be relieved of the work of the *Levite*, but I still should wish to remain the functioning *Kohen*. Indeed, if I follow Jewish tradition, I am in duty bound to continue. You recall the familiar precept in the Ethics of the Fathers: *Ha-amidu talmidim harbeh*, "Raise up many disciples."[9] In a supplementary passage, found in a parallel treatise, Rabbi Akiba adds the interesting precept: "If you have raised many disciples when you are young, do not sit down and say: 'I have done enough,' but raise more disciples in your old age and increase the study of the Torah, because you do not know when you will be more successful."[10] One may be more successful in old age than in youth, in implanting a love for Torah. And

6) Numbers, 8:25.
7) *Ibid.*, 4:47; cf. *ibid.* 1:50; 51; 3:7,8.
8) Malaki, 2:7.
9) Abot, 1:1.
10) Abot d'R Nathan (ed. Schechter), Version II, ch. 4, p. 8a; cf. Genesis Rabbah, 61:3.

so I must follow Rabbi Akiba's injunction. Even though I am now old I must continue to strive to raise disciples. But I need your help for this task.

You may recall that in the Torah lesson of this Sabbath we read: *Mipne sevah takoom v'hadarta pne zaken,* "Thou shalt rise up before the hoary head, and honor the face of the aged."[11] The "hoary head," according to the Rabbis, "refers to one who reaches the age of seventy; while 'the aged' refers to one who reaches the age of sixty."[12] Why this distinction? For the one you have to stand up; for the other you may just honor, respect. When one approaches seventy years, you have to stand up to give him a helping hand!

I am thankful to God that I do not need that helping hand for myself, physically. I am grateful to God that I can still stand on my feet and can see with my eyes. But I would want you to stand up and give me a helping hand in the work of upholding this institution. I am very zealous when it comes to the Brooklyn Jewish Center. I look upon it as a father looks upon his own begotten child — with the same love. I am pained when something unpleasant happens to the Center. I feel happy when all is well with the Center. This institution has blazed a new trail in American Jewish life. Hundreds of communities mention the name Brooklyn Jewish Center with blessedness upon their lips. They speak of it with the highest regard because we have been able to achieve so much. I desire to see it remain on the high pedestal that it has attained. And for that I want your help. And if, dear friends, there is one request that I wish to make of you on this very important milestone in my life, I would say to each and every one of you — paraphrasing the words that the pious Jew says to God every day — *b'yadka afkid ruchi,* "In your hands do I place this Center — part of my very spirit!"

11) Leviticus, 19:32.
12) Abot, 5:24.

Keep that spirit alive. Preserve it! Strengthen it, so that it will continue to infuse the essence of Jewish life in your hearts, in the hearts of your children and children's children, for years and years to come!